# First, it gets worse.

*The chronicles of a Secondary School Behaviour Support Manager*

Randall Skinner

# FOREWORD

I am actually sitting in a lesson as I type this. At the front. Kids are working; some are chatting. One child is looking at his phone on his lap (I hope it's his phone anyway. If it is something else more private, that's a bigger problem and an awkward form to fill out.). Do they really think we can't see when they are looking at their phone in their lap? "Owen, put it away". That will work for both situations, anyway.

I've worked in secondary schools for quite a while now, 17 years to be precise. And pedantic. I trained to change careers and try my hand at a bit of catering. If you're used to kids swearing at you, and parents shouting down the phone, then dealing with a chef is a doddle. However, turns out it's quite difficult to do a proper job when you've only had to work till 4-o-clock your entire adult life, and get 12 weeks of holidays. As my wife would saunter off during the half-term, swanning off to NYC, and I was sweating away in a kitchen for a restaurant full of tourists, I realised that my priorities were poorly placed, to say the least,

I say entire adult life, however, I have also previously been a chef, football coach, barman, film critic, a carer and a call centre worker, so I have also worked with real people, not just teenagers. I think it is so important if you want to be good in the education sector, that you have experienced life a bit before going in to teaching. However, if you are an older teacher who has been a banker for 30 years and you feel like it is your time to "give something back" do not do it. You will hate it and you will be a rubbish teacher. Trust me. I have known some absolutely lovely maths teachers, standing helplessly at the front of the classroom as the paper planes go across the room, shrugging their shoulders and smiling at me. They used to run the board rooms but can't quite tear themselves away from the safety of the teacher desk at the front. School is not like the Bash Street Kids in The Beano; school is like the film Platoon. It is a war zone, if the opposition were full of snot, pent-up aggression, and anything they can possibly find they can make into a weapon (this could be physical or emotional – blackmail, guilt and manipulative actions are all part of the child's arsenal). If you go to school, university, and then straight back into schools, you are probably lacking a bit of a worldview that you are definitely going to need in order to have the thick skin and resilience that can help you bounce back when a kid calls you a fat cunt.

Enjoy these stories from my life and hopefully if you're working at a school you will realise you are not alone...

## One: Rationale: trials, tribulations, reasons vs. excuses

I am not going to mention any staff names, student names, or even school names in this book. I would love to, but I think it is in the best interest of everyone that I don't. Not just due to the embarrassment for any of these people, or the lawsuit I may face, but due to the shocking truth of some of these stories. Frankly, this is my journey from a 24-year-old lazy idiot in to a 37-year-old lazy idiot, albeit a slightly learned one. I am not even sure how I will get on with this book. Undoubtedly, I will get bored during doing this, or read it back and think it is rubbish and delete it all. Nevertheless, here goes. I hope you enjoy it, as I certainly have not. I'm already questioning how much trouble I may get into, and googling solicitors in preparation for the turmoil I may face.

However, the purpose of this book was to show the hard facts of the education sector.

The hilarious stories that happen when you work with kids, the infuriating annoyance of a broken system of the government that has gone on for the last 60 years since the National Curriculum arrived and the cane disappeared, and the heartfelt and truthful feelings that it has caused me to feel. My aim is not to show how hilarious I am. You would likely hate me straight away, and my delicate ego couldn't take it.

I've had some struggles in my life, but I know how lucky I am. I had a lot of potential, full of intelligence, athleticism, opportunity, and decided to do nothing with it. I regret it every day and I feel like now it is too late to do anything about it. I hate myself; I truly do.

I've had some problems with alcohol, self-esteem and issues with addiction throughout my life, and I'm seriously not proud of them. I hate myself for it, but I think you've got that picture now. I have a great family, great friends, but I've thrown my working life away. This is not the platform for a "I could have been a contender" speech but now is when I should say that.

I've had mental health problems and some real lows, and I've decided I'm just going to dedicate my life to others. I'm going to do my best to make sure no one has to have a day feeling worthless like I did for 12 years. Every student that wants my help will get it, and I'm going to make a few people smile along the way. That's what I love the most; making people laugh. However, telling the children 'don't do what I did' doesn't quite cut it with them, though. They expect this message filled with balloons, circus tricks, and stickers. In all fairness, I know how to make balloon animals, and I've got a mean diablo streak, so I'm pretty sure I can nail this.

## 2. Those who can't, teach.

I never wanted to be a teacher. I just enjoy the thought of being a positive influence on students' lives. I think if you can make a difference even in the smallest way you should do it, and that's what I'm doing; making a difference in the smallest way. I did not realise that in doing that, the job also becomes you. Your entire life succumbs to that of the children; you cannot exist as a human being from 8am until 4pm. Any doctor's calls, urgent emails from the mortgage broker, or that need to drink, eat, or pee, all must disappear within those hours, as the children take your entire life away from you. You build a bladder the size of a Mitre Delta.

I'm at an interview at the school I used to attend as a child, and nothing has really changed. Whilst the walls may have a new lick of paint, even the teachers recognise me as the kid who would make fun of them in a lesson, lock them in a cupboard, or missed their lesson due to constantly playing for the football fixtures instead. An awkward smile to those teachers that saw me more than my parents in an evening due to the amount of detentions, makes me realise that a school tour may not be an ideal part of the schedule for me today. Ironically, the job I'm applying for is in a behaviour/isolation room. The two women that I could be working with seem nice. Quite awkward, as one of my mates Dads' is also being interviewed. I hope that I am going to get this but hopefully I'm not causing my mate to get a shit Christmas present. A friend of mine is a head of year here, I've already met my potential boss down the pub, and we got on well. If I'm going to get this, I will be trying to help the worst kids in the school. Trying to teach people (against their will) to be better people and maybe pass English and maths.

As with most schools, I was always going to get that job even before I walked in the door due to my mate already working there and saying that I would do all right. 90% of the time, jobs at schools are already decided before you get there. If you are a maths teacher, you are a 1000% more likely to be promoted due to desperation for you to not leave. Who studies maths at university, to then go into teaching for a meagre salary, instead of banking, marketing, or any other £100,000 job? Only the ones with zero social skills or behaviour management, let me tell you.

Job accepted. I'll start in the new term. Let the journey begin.

*     *     *     *     *

At this point in my life, I was living above a pub. The pub that all my friends go to. The pub that mainly trades in lock-ins. The pub I love. The pub that once closed down for a murder. A pub that once whilst playing darts in a league game, the dart bounced out of double ten only to see on closer inspection that in double 10 was an air rifle pellet. The pub that has been published in FHM at No. 1 as 'Worst Pub in the UK'.

I will tell this one story and then get back to the school stuff.

I'm not quite sure of the how's, whys and wherefores, but somehow, the pub became in the possession of a motorised scooter. Not a moped, but a motorised child's scooter. After hours of messing around with it, generally falling off or crashing it into things, we decided to go a bit "Starsky and Hutch" with it and stack up the empty crisp boxes in to a pyramid and drive the motorised scooter through it as quick as we could. This was exactly how much fun you would think it would be. After we all had several go's, each being more and more elaborate with our dismounts, a drunk man that had been complaining about us decided that he wanted to have a go. We all said that he couldn't, as it was our little game and we didn't want him to break the scooter. All very childish, I know. After a few debates and some quite aggressive language, we decided to give in and let this bloke have a go. During the debates, discussion, and abusive content of the conversation, I was totally unaware that a friend of mine had been moving the empty crisp boxes about 5 foot closer to the wall. Now, I have no idea if you've ever seen a 58-year-old drunken, aggressive man on a motorised scooter drive through a pyramid of empty crisp boxes in to a wall but I would most definitely, highly recommend it.

\* \* \* \* \*

So, first day. New job.

I have been introduced to the students in assemblies that I am the new behaviour support manager. I can see in the kid's eyes that I am tasty lamb to the slaughter in their wolf-like existence. I should probably tell you at this point that I'm 5 ft 11 with a rugby-like frame (albeit alongside the rugby-like ideology of booze, but without the exercise to burn it off). I am aware that I may look like I can handle this lot, but I am most certainly questioning it. This is going to be awful.

If you haven't been into a school in the last 15 years, most secondary schools now have behaviour rooms. Students are sent here if their behaviour is too disruptive for the classroom. A phone call goes to the behaviour room to pick up the child from the classroom, so we go for a quick jog, pick up the student, and bring them back to the behaviour room to settle down, reflect and refresh before re-entering back into normal lessons again. Disruption to the classroom can be subject to opinion, however. At one point I had a phone call to pick up a year 7 girl. When I went to collect her, I saw that she was sat outside, on the floor, completing her maths work. I asked the teacher what she had done wrong, to which the teacher said that she ran out of desks. The poor kid was in tears, completely confused as to why she had been chucked out, and the scary 'behaviour manager' has come to get her. I asked the teacher to clarify a little more. She explained "well, I've only got 29 desks, and I have 30 children. She cannot come in, so you must take her away."

We have a big open plan room. There is an area where students are placed if they have been removed from lessons for distracting others from working, and a separate room where students have caused bigger issues and are in for up to what could be a week. This is like an internal exclusion; you don't get to see your friends at break or lunch, and you're basically excluded from the rest of school, but you have to complete work in silence. To add to this humiliation, the All-Day room is centred in the middle of this entire area, and is partitioned by glass. It is very much like watching monkeys during feeding time. I was based most frequently in the main room with the "all-dayers" to start with. The behaviour is awful when I am in there, and no matter how much you might shout at them, it doesn't change the way these students behave; I may as well not be here. If I took my shirt off and started singing Mysterious Girl these kids wouldn't notice. I come home a broken man. However, luckily, my home is a pub. You see where my alcoholic ways provided me with a sense of sanity from a tiresome and draining day with the worst kids in the school. Who are likely to be the ones setting fire to the McDonalds down the road about now.

### 3 - "OI, SIR"

Off to London today to watch football with my mates and put this horrible job behind me for a day or two. The problem with working in the same town as your school is that you are undoubtedly going to bump into kids. To add to this, the kids I work with are genuinely looking to show off to their friends. I'm with my friends too but luckily a few of my friends work in schools and so they understand the pain of bumping into students when you are out. They're also good enough to hide the tinnies when you walk past the students. The problem is, you cannot put an abusive kid into detention when they are out of uniform. You can definitely see where this is going can't you.

As I'm waiting for my train. Here he comes. Bowling down the stairs of the train platform, the worst kid in our school.

"OI SIR!"

Here we go.

"YOU CAN'T DO ANYTHING BECAUSE WE'RE NOT IN SCHOOL" he bellowed at me, laughing and guffawing to his mates.

"Nice to see you," I lie.

"YOU'RE A FUCKING WANKER SIR" (love how he still added Sir, a sign of respect, despite the beautiful use of an adjective to the term wanker. I'd love to share that with his English teacher at some point).

I was actually quite amazed he was still going with "Sir" but I think that had probably more to do with the fact he had forgotten my name.

"YOU'RE A FUCKING WANKER!" he repeated, just to make sure his mates had heard, waiting to see what I might do next.

People are beginning to look over, and I have nowhere to go with this. There are no police around and I'm stuck on a busy train platform being called a "fucking wanker" by a 13-year-old skinhead. Options are quickly dwindling, and I'm looking down the train line begging for my train to turn up.

"YOU'RE A FUCKING…"

My SLT friend (assistant headteacher for want of a better term) from another school has come to my rescue. He picks this kid up by the loop on the top of his six-quid rucksack and says in a quiet calm voice.

"If you say another word to my pal you're going on those fucking tracks".

The kid is squirming around trying to get free and runs off.

I'm so appreciative of my mate for this, and unbelievably happy that the kid has gone. I'm just glad I won't be getting into any trouble for swearing at kids in public. In my very green and uncertain attitude to this whole new job, I have no idea what I would do next time, if I'm on my own.

Back at school on Monday, of course, I'm lucky enough to bump into this wonderful child. When you work in the behaviour room, you only really get to see a handful of kids, but they are by far the ones you don't actually want to see at all. The kid tells me, "Your mate is a fucking wanker!" I responded quite smugly with, "He shut you up though didn't he?". I reported him to his head of year for saying "fucking wanker" in school. This time I can nail him. His punishment? A day in the behaviour room with me. I've learnt a lot from this!

## 4 - Professionalism Getting Loose

A friend of mine who basically got me this job, has asked if I would like to give up my half-term and go to Devon with him to go surfing. I'm up for a laugh with him. He said it will be fun, but fails to mention that we are going with ten other staff and 112 students. Despite this unforeseen circumstance, I feel like this might be the best idea. If I stay at home, I will be in the pub for the entire week, start drinking when it opens until when it closes, until those lines eventually blur.

Off to Bideford I go.

Coach journeys can be horrible when you are with a load of adults, let alone kids. Add to that, we go with the cheapest quote; that is, no air-conditioning, and very little space for a fully-grown man with restless legs. I vow to myself I will never go on another one of these. The way these kids are treating this coach is a total disgrace. There are more sweets on the floor than I have ever eaten in my life. The noise, the smell; the vomit after the constant sweet-eating. Never again.

We stop at the services to rethink our choices in life and give the coach driver an extremely well-earned cigarette break.

As we are counting the students back on to the coach, we see a female Head of Year shouting at three students to hurry up and get on the coach. It's only at the steps we realise that these three students do not attend our school. Thankfully we manage to chivvy them along and back to their own school groups without anyone realising.

The activity centre is alright, and the students are incredibly excited. Judging by all the Red Bull cans, this could be a long night (new lesson: remove all energy drinks from students before we start the trip). We are still winding up the Head of Year, calling her the "child catcher". She has asked that this nickname does not catch on when we get back home.

As soon as we arrive, the "Old Pros'" are straight into the staff room, filling the various fridges with booze and houmous. The Head of Sixth Form has come with a special treat for us... a Nintendo Wii. This has become a massive divider between the young and old staff. The older staff are trying to have intellectual conversations whilst the younger staff are trying to not fall off Rainbow Road. Not sure where the kids are at this point; hopefully the activity staff are wearing them out before bedtime.

The Head of Year 7 (old) is not happy that the Wii is in use and one night, she has thrown down the gauntlet and has complained that we are spending too much time in the evenings playing on the Wii. The young staff are ignoring her, but you can see the tension building and when you are told off by an older teacher, they do have the habit of talking to you like a child in their class, which is infuriating when you are 24.

She is speaking about books and has asked a young art teacher who is playing Super Smash brothers what his favourite book is, in a loud condescending tone.

You can cut the tension with a knife.

"1984", he replies, trying to cut the conversation short.

"Oh? Why's that?" asked the inquisitive Head of Year, trying to take his eyes off the screen.

"Because people just sit around all day watching FUCKING TELE!"

The room falls silent for about five minutes, followed by some sniffles, and the Head of Year has gone to bed. She must have heard the laughter after she left the room. That probably has not improved matters. Can't wait for the awkward chat across the breakfast table.

The trip flies by and fun is had by all. One evening we are manning the corridors, checking students are in their rooms and going to sleep. There is a lot of talk in one of the boy's bedrooms. We stop and listen for a minute or two just outside the door, before telling everyone to be quiet. After visiting a few other rooms, the girls have complained that the boys have been knocking on their door and running away (standard). After a few more check-ins, we go back to our little staff room and crack open a beer. After about 20 minutes, some girls have knocked on our door to tell us about the boys knocking on their door and turning the lights on again. We go to the boy's room and get all ten of them out of bed to tell them off.

An hour later, the girls are there again with the same problem. All boys are back in the corridor and being told off again. My mate has the great idea of ringing all of their parents in a row in front of them at midnight to tell them their sons are misbehaving. This is genius. My mate is now backing out of this plan and the rest of us are aware that our fearless trip leader is slurring a bit after seven gin and tonics. He comes up (without telling the rest of us) with a clever plan to pretend to ring one kids parents and then give them the "How did that make you feel?" speech.

This plan was expertly put in place and would have worked perfectly, if it was not for the phone ringing halfway through his pantomimed rant.

Despite this slightly awkward moment, one kid has broken, sobbing. We all feel a little bit bad but enjoy the rest of our evening without any further interruption.

It is coming to the end of the rainiest week of our lives and I've been tasked today of trying to take photos of students smiling and having fun. I fail, as they aren't doing either. They are all tired and they've had enough. At one point I run in to the woods as I see a group cycling; it's after about 20 photos and a member of staff stopping me that I realise these kids are from another group.

The journey home from rainy Bideford takes almost ten hours. When we eventually arrive home the parents don't appear too happy with us. Clearly the insanely awful traffic was our fault and we should be scolded due to putting them out like this.

All students are taken home... except one. There's always one. Desperately trying to ring his Mum now, and not 30 minutes ago when we repeatedly told him to, and he assured us that he had. We sit and wait for Mum for 45 minutes after a ten-hour coach journey, Mum arrives and takes her son without any apology. Or gratitude for that matter. I decide to get the kid in trouble next week for his Mum's rudeness. I'm sure I can find a way.

Monday comes around and they thank us in the briefing for giving up our time. That is it! Working pro-rata, I am not paid for my holidays, but a thank-you in front of everyone by the Head who pronounces my name wrong is all I get.

I must say that since vowing never to do an activity trip again, I then continue with another ten, one every single year, and even running them myself (but not before a few anxiety-induced vomits before we jump on the coach). I learned that confiscating the sweets at the start of the trip and keeping them 'safe' at the front with the teachers was the ideal situation to ensure a safe and satisfying trip for all. It also helped to keep the sugar levels of the driver going.

## 5 - Tell me why I don't like Sundays?

I've had a massive session on the booze and I've woken up at 11am! I panic and ring the Absence Hotline straight away. I'm incredibly surprised but relieved, that it has gone through to voicemail. I make up some excuse that I had to go to hospital as to why I couldn't call earlier.

I would have got away with this. However, I think I'm going to end up in trouble... it's Sunday.

Another meeting with the headteacher for unprofessionalism. This one is coming with my first warning as well. Fair enough.

\* \* \* \* \*

I've expressed an interest in helping out with the school football teams and P.E have literally jumped on me. I now help run fixtures pretty much every Saturday morning. The teams are doing okay, even if they aren't that good. I have one player who has cerebral palsy. I'm keen for him to play and have the same opportunity as everyone else, so I speak to the manager of the opposing team and tell him about my player, and ask him to tell his players not to kick him up in the air; he says he'll do his best.

After around an hour, I bring the cerebral palsy student on, and give the other schools PE teacher/manager a nod, to remind him of my disabled player.

I am refereeing too, and we are five-maybe-six-nil down. I give a very soft penalty in the last couple of minutes to us and the captain decides that our player with cerebral palsy should take it.

Boom! He runs up and smashes it into the top corner. The lads go absolutely wild. It is absolute scenes! He's up on their shoulders and they are celebrating. I start crying, I cannot believe it; it is probably the best thing I have ever seen on a football pitch; it is like watching 1000 'US soldiers returning from war and seeing their children' videos on YouTube. I walk towards their manager, having to compose myself, and he has a massive smile on his face. Without me having to say a word, he says, "That is what school football is all about". I hold that thought with me at every game I coach, ref, or manage.

At the end of the game, I tidy up and put all the kit in the wash, make sure we have the correct number of balls and corner flags that we started with, and wait for all the students to leave so I can lock up the changing rooms. When the penalty scorer leaves, I stop him and tell him just how he filled me with pride, and how his goal made me incredibly happy, and something that I will remember forever. I plan to ring home and perhaps send a letter to his parents. I continue and say, "All the lads celebrating with you was good, wasn't it?"

He replied, "I don't know why they did that... I scored two last week." He toddled off with a smile and a "see ya, Sir - thanks!".

\*     \*     \*     \*     \*

I've popped to my local shops with my current girlfriend, and a group of my students have decided to follow me back to her flat. She has a son and I worry about her having nuisance knock-and-runs and over-eager trick-or-treaters, or having to clean egg off her windows. Or clean something else off her windows. Who knows.

I walk the 20 metres back to them and ask them politely to go away as it's not fair to harass teachers out of school. I stay polite and say I look forward to seeing them on the Monday.

They continue to follow but from a further distance, hiding behind cars and around corners, and I'm getting fairly annoyed.

I approach the lads again and say, "This will be a police matter if you follow me to my house. Now do me a favour and piss off!". I'm annoyed that I swore at them, but I needed them to know I was serious. Standing and waiting to ring the police for a bunch of lads who will eventually just run away would be an incredible waste of everyone's time.

I arrive back to school on Monday and straight in the headteacher's office to hear that there has been a complaint made from a parent about me swearing at their kids. I explain the situation, but I am still handed a verbal warning. Whilst I understand, I still think this is unfair, given the way in which the children were harassing me outside of school. I get the impression that this headteacher has now had enough of me, and is doing his best to get rid of me swiftly and easily.

(Parents are always right in school, and Senior Leadership are too scared about parents "going to the papers" about anything. Most parents are really great and supportive but many are actually idiots, and make our lives very difficult indeed).

\* \* \* \* \*

I have a party this weekend and no money. Luckily, it's the World Cup and I set up an elaborate sweepstake costing £10 a team. I have a month to pay this back. Party on.

\* \* \* \* \*

My best friend has asked me to help him out in our local shopping centre, to hand out flyers for his new football coaching business. Sadly, this isn't as random as it sounds. He has done sessions before that has involved me dressed up as a 7-foot teddy bear trying to save penalties.

It is a really hot, horrible job, but he's said he will buy me a few pints for it, so I obviously say yes. I worry about being spotted in the town centre by students, but the bear is pretty all-encompassing, and no-one will ever know that it's me.

Quite a few students walk past me, obviously not knowing it is me. I hand out flyers and badges, pose for selfies and hug toddlers, while my friend talks to parents about coaching sessions. Something had to happen though, and here comes one of the rudest kids in year 11 coming over shouting,

"HES NOT A REAL BEAR! LOOK YOU CAN SEE HIS HANDS AND TRAINERS!"

I put my arm around him and whisper,

"SHUT THE FUCK UP STANLEY!"

Stanley is incredibly confused whilst walking away.

Monday morning arrives, and I see Stanley at the school gates. When I ask him how his weekend was, he seems a little perplexed. I drop a few hints that perhaps I might have been around, when he was having a nice hug with a footballing bear... he still seems incredibly confused. God bless the thick ones.

## 6 - "But Sir! She used to babysit Captain Tom!"

Really struggling with getting in to work today. I feel like a stiff breeze could knock me down; I feel like crying and I could go at any moment. The smallest thing today could send me over the edge. I've had enough of this life.

I am always amazed by what the presence of someone else, who isn't a teacher, can do to a classroom. For example, if you are showing around visitors. When you go in to a class they normally behave impeccably for those two minutes. This is really handy when it comes to Ofsted. This sadly does not work for all students, as a student has had to be removed today by telling a potential new head of science not to work here, as it is shit. To be fair, he was on the money.

\* \* \* \* \*

The same child has been sent to me again today. He is an absolute nightmare but I think he is great; he is totally hilarious. One of our male teachers has white hair in a ponytail and makes a good lookalike for Dracula; this lad has made a fairly decent crucifix out of two rulers (glue, 2 non-shatter rulers, Tippex and a brown Pen).

He's been sent to us today for an absolute blinder.

Whilst queueing to get in to his lesson he has begun to mess around with some other students who are walking past. He's thrown one to the ground and is now beginning to pretend to wee on him. The 70-something-year-old LSA (learning support assistant) has shouted at him to "Act your age!". His reply was "I would say the same thing to you, but you would die." As the LSA tells me this, I am struggling not to cry with laughter and am quite happy and relieved that she is leaving the room.

*    *    *    *    *

Really under the cosh today. We must have had 25-or-so students who have been asked to leave lessons today. I am feeling the pressure. One of our jobs is to also provide the student support centre with work (I don't understand why - they have about fifteen people over there, and there's only three of us.). It's an absolute madhouse and some kids are quite literally swinging from the rafters. We can't get hold of any SLT, so we are just fighting fire after fire, and soon enough, I'm sure we will literally start fighting fires. The phone rings again and I have no idea where we can place another student. It's the head of the student support centre, wanting work for a student. I start to tell her that there is no chance because of how busy we are. This doesn't seem to deter her from telling me why it is necessary to keep students in the SSC busy and how busy they are with... I've hung up. I warn my boss to expect a complaint within the next five minutes.

\* \* \* \* \*

A student who is from quite a disadvantaged and vulnerable family is extremely proud of his chilli con carne that he's made today in his DT food lesson and is coming up to our office to show us what he's made. He is so chuffed, as it is the first time he's cooked anything, and he is planning to feed his family tonight with it. We see him quite often up here, as he's quite a naughty boy at times. On his way up to our office, devastatingly, he trips and drops it, right outside the headteacher's office. Chilli has spilled out of the broken plastic

Tupperware, and the young man is so upset that he's turned into the Hulk. The headteacher's PA is all of a fluster. With the mess in front of her, she has started to shout at the lad to clear it up. By the time I get there, the boy is fighting back tears and the heads' PA has begun to raise her voice quite sternly. I ask if everything is okay and the heads' PA tells me clearly that this mess needs cleaning up quickly!

The boy, now fully crying, looks at her and screams "Why don't you just shut up you silly old cunt?!" It is a shame I'll never see this kid again for that because I think he was dead right. I would have slipped him a tenner to get his family a takeaway if I'd managed to, before he was scooped up and quickly escorted off school site.

\* \* \* \* \*

As part of the behaviour department, we have a supply of spare uniform to lend to students if they have financial difficulties, or they have just simply forgotten parts of their uniform. It's amazing how many children, despite years of wearing a tie, don't realise they are missing it until tutor time. Before you question why we are allowing children to wear dirty, second-hand uniform, let me make this clear. All of the uniform is brand new, and washed after every time it is worn. This is the regular phone call I get from angry parents, insisting their child shouldn't be wearing 'used clothes'.

A girl has arrived with us today, and she has brand spanking new white trainers on. She (obviously!?!) can't be in lessons, so she has to stay with us, or borrow some spare shoes. She is kicking off massively about this and is flat-out refusing to wear our spare shoes. We find the underlying cause of this; on her way to school today she stood in a heap of dog poo and then neatly disposed of her dirty school shoes in a hedge. I've asked her where they are, and she has given me some rough directions. I go looking for these shoes, figuring I could probably follow the scent like a hound. Lo and behold, the aroma of the shoes is pretty strong, and they are found fairly easily. For the greater good, I will get this sorted and get her back in to her lessons. Without good teacher interaction in lessons, students just aren't learning; when they are frustrated for being based in the behaviour room all day due to their uniform infractions, they then tend to kick off even more, leading to extra time for poor behaviour. That makes it sound like a prison; it's not far off, although the kids haven't quite worked out how to hide drugs in the bricks. I don't think.

I get the shoes back to school and wipe the dog mess off them, retching the entire time. I have a lot of previous experience of dealing with poo (severely autistic adults' poo to be precise), so I can normally handle it well, but the smell is unreal. I genuinely look at myself in the mirror at this point and say loudly... "this is your job". This has to be a new low.

She returns to lessons with clean shoes and without saying thank you.

*     *     *     *     *

Feeling worthless today. I find a moment to have a little cry in the toilet and try my hardest to not make any noise as someone else comes in the toilet. I would go for a walk to sort myself out but there isn't the time. There is just more and more shit to deal with. More students, more targets, more SLT and more complaints.

*     *     *     *     *

A student has come to us saying that he is being bullied. Apparently, some students have made an online dating profile 'for' him and are subsequently taking the mickey. He is furious. I ask him who is actually bullying him and he gives me a few names. I find one of the 'bullies' and ask him about it and if he has anything on his phone. He compliantly hands over his phone, and I spot a few screen shots of the profile. I reference the profile against the lad who is being bullied. It seems that the person who has set it up has not only used quite a nice picture of him, but also guessed the boys date of birth correctly. I'm not sure how the app works myself, or whether we can delete his profile. I just want to ensure he doesn't feel bullied anymore. I use the head of years' Facebook account and set up the app on her phone, as I am yet to afford a phone that can do this. Just to test this out, I sign her up, and swipe right on a few lads I reckon might suit her well. She can thank me later. Once I've navigated my way around the app, I realise that the boy has obviously set it up himself and is now trying to save face. I tell him to delete it and talk to him about internet safety. If he gets bullied again, he should come straight to me. Poor sod.

## 7 - Question 1. Who shouldn't have drunk so much?

There is a quiz night on tonight at the school. It has been organised by the PTFA (Parent Teachers and Friends Association I think). The quiz is awful. It is taking too long and considering I have been drinking since midday and it is now nine-o-clock, I am way too drunk to be at a school function. I have already insulted my mate because I thought it was funny, and now I'm moving on to others on my team, who I don't particularly know very well. Someone should really be stopping me at this point.

The questions are really long and tenuously linked to the inane chatter and I am beginning to tell the quizmaster this from 20 yards away. I am a total embarrassment and no one wants to be near me. I can tell, as there is a groan in the room when I return from the toilet. Here is an example of a question: Andy Dufrane was a character in the Shawshank Redemption, who was played by Tim Robbins, in a book written by Stephen King. Name the current King of Monaco. Are you kidding me?!

The booze is cheap, the quiz is ridiculous, it's got even worse and so have I. I've already been sick in the disabled toilet. Unfortunately, I feel like this is a good thing, as I will now have more room for more alcohol, and a little less bloated. By the end of the night, I've upset the majority of people in the hall, most of the staff I work with, and I'm lying awake in my mate's bed. He has a massive go at me and he's not wrong, as I have no idea how I am here.

Monday. I'm back in the heads office again, apologising. I give him some sob story about my life and he says I need help. He offers me a website to get my drinking sorted out and I thank him massively. I leave his office thinking, "I've got away with that, which will be a funny story to tell down the pub later". Probably not the outcome that the head was looking for.

* * * * *

I'm on lunch duty today. My wage is pretty poor; so poor that I need to supplement it with some extra duties. I start work at 8am, and finish at 4.30pm, with a 50 minute lunch break in the middle. I give up my lunch break every day to take on a duty, monitoring the students, dealing with any problems, etc.

It seems a little quiet today, so I have a little wander around the site. As I get to the outdoor changing rooms, I swear to you about fifty kids, all smoking, go sprinting away from me. There is literally no way of me reporting all these students to their heads of year. I report it to the people who can check the CCTV and name a few kids who I could kind of guess were there.

* * * * *

There is something happening out on the field. There is a large group surrounding a couple of students. This normally means a fight, so I get a jog on and get into the middle of the crowd, and find a boy in the middle, holding a pigeon. I ask him to release the pigeon but he's told me there is something wrong with him and he won't fly. I ask him again to leave the pigeon alone whilst my colleague tries to move the large group on. The lad with the pigeon yells, "BE FREE!" and throws the pigeon in the air. The pigeon, with literally no movement, smashes to the ground with an almighty thud. The student looks a little shocked and saddened. I clear the students away from the area and head off to get a cardboard box from reprographics. When I arrive back, there are now 20 or 30 students around this pigeon, on their way to a PE lesson. I scoop the pigeon in to the box and start walking down the other end of the field to place the pigeon in to the woods, let him recover, or let natural selection take its' place. I turn to see these 30 students still watching what I am doing from about 100 metres away. I quietly tip the pigeon into the woods and continue on pretending that the pigeon is still in the box.

I put the box on the floor and shrug my shoulders dramatically, before stamping on this box as hard as I can. I was jumping up and down and then started kicking it towards the woods. All I could hear was an almighty "NOOOOOOOOOOOO!" coming from the crowd a hundred metres away. I chuckled to myself as I strolled back to the buildings with a well-destroyed cardboard box.

Later on, I did tell them the truth.

\* \* \* \* \*

It's the afternoon, when things start to get extra busy, as students have just pumped themselves full of sugar once more ready for their next lesson. I get a call to say a student is missing from his lesson. As I get to the toilets nearby, I smell smoke, and really hope this is not an actual fire. Of course, the absconding student is in the toilet, smoking. I open the door ajar, stand at the doorway and tell him to get out. After a while, he leaves and I ask him to hand over his cigarettes, which he does. He swears blind that he was not smoking in the toilets, even though smoke is visibly hugging the ceiling. I call his Mum to tell her that her son has been caught smoking at school, but I can tell she doesn't really care. She tells me to destroy the cigarettes as she can't be bothered to come and collect them. Therefore, I do... one at a time... over a period of a few days.

## 8. Fix, fiddle, re-draw, conspiracy

The annoying IT guy has not been in for a while, which is frustrating as my computer screen appears fuzzy. I nip down to his office to see that his PC is missing. I really hope this doesn't mean what we all know it does mean. Lo and behold, he doesn't return to the school, and a few rumours get around the school in regarding to 'struck off' and 'barred from the DBS register'. Fuck.

(I am telling a few gruesome stories, but these have all genuinely happened throughout my time at what people perceive to be quite a normal good school).

\*     \*     \*     \*     \*

I have been asked to be in a school "Teachers have Talent" competition to raise money for Comic Relief. I say yes and when it comes to it, I am actually quite nervous. There's no denying that I don't mind a laugh, or a bit of attention here and there, but when it comes to the crunch, I'm petrified of being shit. There are about 300 students in this hall and I am about ten minutes away from break dancing in front of them. I mentioned my fairly large rugby frame; this may come as a bit of a shock to the students.

The head goes on first (obviously) and starts playing his acoustic guitar with a lot of cheese. The kids look incredibly bored and annoyed they are watching this in their lunch break. You can tell that they may have seen this "cool headteacher act" a few too many times already. In fact I'm pretty sure he's played his guitar at every assembly he leads, once a year, with a rendition of Mustang Sally.

An English teacher performs a song, which he has written himself about salad. It is actually quite good and gets a good amount of cheers from the students.

Right. I'm up.

I 'struggle' from the back of the stage, knocking over some things with crutches that I borrowed from a mate. I make sure I'm making a real racket. I arrive on stage and use the crutches to limp out in front of the students. I say I'm going to perform my favourite song, 'Angels' by Robbie Williams. (Note: This is of course, not my favourite song.)

"I sit and wait... right stop, stop... STOP! I need absolute silence for this! Some of you are being incredibly rude!" I'm building up my confidence now.

I do this twice more before winking to the drama teacher to play 'Bound 4 Da Reload' by Oxide and Neutrino. I ditch the crutches and start one of the worst performances of break dancing that anyone has ever seen. I throw in a worm, a windmill, and a few other moves I have seen Usher perform with ease (all unpractised and dangerous to an obese borderline alcoholic male). During this performance, I remember that I have never performed these moves sober.

I get a standing ovation from the kids and think I'm a shoe-in for 'Teachers got Talent' champion.

I go back on to duty, horrifically out of breath and suitably embarrassed as to what I had just done.

I go back to the hall for the results only to lose out to the two fit heads of drama and English who mimed to Telephone by Lady Gaga and Beyoncé. I'm overwhelmed with anger. I was absolutely robbed.

*  *  *  *  *

A call from the head and he wants me to come down to his office. I wait outside like a naughty student, heart racing, and walk into his office. I thought this was going to be a good meeting as I felt like I hadn't done anything wrong for a while. How wrong I was! I walk in to an absolute tsunami of a man screaming at me for all sorts of reasons; apparently I told a kid to shut up (probably). Apparently I taught a kid the sign bullshit in sign language (definitely), and to top it all off, apparently I gave a student a high five in the corridor. "What's wrong with that?" I ask. Wow, I've never seen a man go redder quicker and he screams in my face asking me, "Are you on some kind of power trip?" I reply, "Shouting in someone's face for a high-five? Yeah... it's me on a power trip." I am given a written warning and I am basically being told to pack my bags. I feel absolutely rotten, and I think everything I've started to work towards over the last few months is being taken away from me.

It is a long night, in which I decide I should probably move out of the pub for my own good and possibly stop living life like it may end tomorrow. That, and the doctor telling me that I have a slightly fatty liver.

**9. ARD-ly Working**

Its parent's day at school. Our school does this slightly differently to a lot of schools. Rather than parents' evenings, we cancel all lessons for the day, and parents make appointments with the form tutor throughout the day, to talk through the school report, set some targets, and raise any concerns. These days are incredibly boring for support staff. My entire job revolves around students being in school. When they're not in school, I don't have a whole lot to do, and the school tend to forget about support staff. We potter around and talk to our mates. The year 11s are selling coffee all day in order to fundraise for their upcoming prom, but it's free to staff members (although they still get paid from the school for providing us with refreshments). Therefore, we keep ourselves alert and energised with an incredible amount of limitless, free coffee, which we would never normally have chance to slurp cold on a normal school day. I tend to bump into some old friends as their children go to the school, but at 4-o-clock I'm absolutely thrilled, as the boredom has eventually ended. I'm a little smug leaving at 4, when the teaching staff are still running appointments until 7pm.

\*     \*     \*     \*     \*

We have a new teacher at school. She is Indian, just under 4ft and will be eaten alive by the students. Whilst it's great to have a wide cultural breadth in the school staff, students use this as any opportunity to be 'casually racist', attempting to 'not understand' what she is saying, claiming she 'smells of curry', and generally running rings around her until she fails.

This obviously makes my job a lot harder, as I will be in and out of there like an English batsman. Straight away, the students are on form. Lazy impressions, saying things like "Where we come from!" and some aroma-based comments. It is truly awful to hear, and the students are torn a new one, whilst we call parents too (being in a fairly white British town doesn't really help, the parents encourage them, and leave me helpless on the phone when trying to explain the inappropriate behaviour of their child).

Students always give the 'new teacher' a hard time, so they normally settle in and after a while, the students sort themselves out and start to fall into line. This could also be the case for this teacher, if she was any good. Sadly, she is not. On the white board (sorry, 'wipe board'), the sums are calculated wrongly and only the bottom third of the board is being used due to the lack of steps. Students are being thrown out of there left, right and centre and there is nothing we can do to stop it. Outside of all the racist behaviour, sadly this woman is a terrible teacher and should not be in the industry. She is receiving no support from her faculty and definitely no support from SLT. She will basically be here until she cannot handle it anymore, which is incredibly sad to watch. She will get ill. She will do something stupid like lash out in front of the children. Alternatively, just a full on breakdown in front of the kids. I've seen both before. It can get ugly. We have tried supporting her by being in her lessons but a) you cannot tell her to go whilst you take over the lesson, and b) if you told her to go, she would not understand. The way it works is just like the pigeon in the box: she will be "naturally selected" to leave at some point and end up at worse and worse schools, until she gives up the career entirely.

A student has arrived at my door and is crying. She tells me the Indian teacher has sent her there. I ask what she had done. "She sent me here because I have wet eyes!" Now. Children lie. All the time! Little white ones and massive horrible life changing ones. Especially when it comes to behaviour at schools. You can ask, "Why are you here?" and they will respond very innocently with, "Oh, it's because I sat on a bench wrong", and when you get to the bottom of it, you hear that sitting on a bench wrong involved assaulting three other students, jumping on the bench, and breaking it before spitting in the teachers face. Therefore, I did not believe this student for one second.

"Aren't all eyes wet?" I reply.

"She said it's because I have wet eyes!" she repeated.

I go to the lesson and ask to speak to the teacher outside. I ask her why the student is with me. Low and behold, it is due to wet eyes.

She was a little upset in the lesson and other students were asking her "What's wrong?" and "Are you okay?", to the point the teacher put her in a detention and threw her out.

I never really worked out the reason why she was upset; I left that to the very lovely girls I worked with; I just gave her a few silly jokes until the sniffles stopped and there were a few grins, and I left her to it. I tell the student to sit with me and do some homework until the lesson is over and cancel her detention. I e-mail SLT to raise my concerns about the teacher; she will still be here next year.

    \*  \*  \*  \*  \*

We have a briefing about a new student who has Tourette's syndrome along with ADHD. He is an incredibly positive, lovely kid. Really top notch. I walk in to his Science lesson to ask his teacher if he had any problems with a tricky student from a prior lesson.

"FUCKING LOSER!"

I see the kids with Tourette's is in here.

\* \* \* \* \*

A student is in our 'All Day Room' and is upset about the rumours that are circulating about him throughout the school. I tell him not to worry about it; he is safe with us and no one will bother him where he is. We do our best to get information from him and how best we can help him at school. At this point, an idiot LSA enters looking for our student. She says, "Are you Brian?" The child nods. "There is a kid called Gary downstairs who wants to beat you up!" Brian bellows "WHERE IS HE!" and runs out of the door looking for Gary. I launch out of my chair and pelt down the stairs to try to stop this fight. At the top of the stairs, I pause to tell this 65-year-old woman "Could you be any more of a fucking idiot?". Expect another complaint – but come on!

\* \* \* \* \*

I have been asked to accompany a group of sixth formers to London for a geography trip. It's a lecture with seven students that no other staff member will go on. I am told I have to go, with the extra initiative of £15 for lunch. The travel doesn't take long, and it's a day away from the bunch of nightmare kids, so I'm in.

I spend every penny of the money at Burger King whilst the students sit in the lecture hall. I also buy a copy of four–four-two magazine to tide me over for the second half of the lecture. It is a long, boring day. There are times when I think my job is difficult as I'm no good with time on my own. I understand I am not a coal miner, or working on an oil rig, but during this lecture, I would prefer to be a toilet cleaner. Not a person who cleans toilets but an actual thing you clip on to your toilet.

On the way home a friend walks past our train and knocks on the window. My stomach sinks because this mate... is an idiot. He stands near me, not realising that the other five people I am sitting with are all sixth formers from my school. He starts telling me about a fight he got in the other week, when he was out of his face on drink and drugs, before I introduce him to my students, just so he knows to shut the fuck up.

I return to school embarrassed with the company I keep, and then angry as the school won't refund my Burger King as I have lost the receipt.

## 10. Check, Delete, Repeat.

I have just started dating one of the teachers. She's great and completely out of my league and does not know about my drinking problems; everything is going great so far. She lives a fair way away from the town, so I get to go on fun dates in London with her. Life seems to be going pretty smoothly right now.

*   *   *   *   *

A plane has landed on the school field. It genuinely requires a double take. A two-seater biplane has landed on the field and I am doing my best to get this guy moving. It is 8.40am, and the students were just on their way to tutor time, some of whom were walking across the field at the time. I'm pretty sure this hasn't come up in any risk assessments before.

The pilot is looking extremely confused (we are all feeling the same right about now) and I ask him what on earth is going on. He has ran out of fuel heading to a local airfield and has decided to be safe and land on our field. I turn to see every student in the school looking out of the window. This is going to be an incredibly busy day for me, as not one kid will work today.

\* \* \* \* \*

A student in year 10 has come to me to complain that several year 7 students are bullying him. I explain to him that if you have a briefcase and mackintosh coat, with a flask of coffee trudging through the corridors, and The Independent tucked beneath your arm each morning, this will inevitably lead to some bullying. He didn't seem to understand this concept. I agree that he is allowed to be the person that he wishes to be; however, I'm now going to have to go and tell off the several students for, in my opinion, quite rightly bullying an older student, for blatant weirdness.

\* \* \* \* \*

IT'S A SNOW DAY! I am looking out the window begging for this snow to start settling. As a worker at a school, you either want tonnes of snow and a day off, or zero snow whatsoever.

I wake up in the morning to see my worst nightmare. An inbetweenie. Not enough snow for a day off, but enough to be bombarded by wet icy slush bombs all day. The problem with snowballs is that it is incredibly hard to pinpoint who has thrown it. The head gives us a big speech about "business as usual" and "no snowballs".

That means, we have to reprimand any child that we see throw a snowball. This is the worst job of all. The Snow Nazi.

Kids are just looking out of the window all day longingly, asking the same questions: how much snow is needed for a day off? If only we knew...

I go to my break duty on the playground to see approximately 80 students throwing and kicking snow at each other. After ten minutes, the head is on my shoulder telling me to stop them all before walking off. "Thanks for your help," I mutter. I continue to be pelted with slush bombs, as I 'firmly encourage' the students that 'it's time to go inside now'.

\* \* \* \* \*

One of the younger, attractive female teachers has been found on Instagram, not wearing a lot of clothes; it's doing the rounds on students' phones. One of those problems you just love to deal with, every day. It is a regular incident that students are part of: 'sexting'. No matter how many assemblies, conversations, warnings you give, students always seem to get themselves in these situations. It's quite a surprise when the tables are turned, and you are going through the student's phones for an indecent image of a teacher. Every male student is trying to get copies and due to social media, it's been shared everywhere.Our job for the rest of the day entails walking around the school, collecting people's phones and deleting the photo off it, followed by asking who they received this from, and who they have now sent it to. Check, delete, repeat. This will take all day. The teacher is incredibly upset, so she won't get in trouble, yet this is 100% her fault, and I'm pretty sure is a sackable offence.

The students kept being told how inappropriate it is to circulate photos and yet here we are. You cannot blame them; you would be showing this photo around when you were at school. I feel sorry for every kid whose phone we have to go through; as soon as you start searching through students phones, you realise this glamorous photograph of a teacher is the least of our problems.

\* \* \* \* \*

I have been asked to cover a lesson. I have no work, no computer, and no idea. I've never really had to teach a lesson before; I normally just deal with the worst child, and remove, like a superhero to the teachers. I dig through my memory banks and remember a maths lesson from when I was once at school, and decide to wing it. I tell the kids something I like and something I dislike, and everything I like has a theme. The theme today is going to be double letters. For example, I like football, but I don't like rugby; and so on. When a student feels like they have made the connection, they can join in and say something that they like and dislike. A few of them have worked it out early and I am telling them more and more about how much I like Mississippi. The ones who haven't got it are getting angrier and angrier and not one of them has thought to write down any of this, as they would have got it instantly.

The students know what football team I support and have just plainly asked if I like Delle Alli?

They may have found a glitch in this matrix. "Yes I like Delle Alli"

"What about Harry Kane, Sir?" I end the game and they do silent reading.

\* \* \* \* \*

Its trip time again and we are back off to Devon for an activity week. After complaining about it last time, I feel that it is a good opportunity to not pay for food for a week.

A student has arrived early for the coach and his Dad has asked if he has to sign anything. I tell him no and he leaves. That is it - he leaves! He didn't even say goodbye to his son; just got in his car and went. I decide that this kid is going to have the best week of his life. I make sure he wins every competition and prize going. At the last night's evening activities, the disco, he's on my shoulders, having a whale of a time. I know this kid doesn't have the best of times at home, and I want to provide him with a male role model that he can follow. I make him the 'King of the Trip', and on saying goodbye, he is sobbing. This kid is going under my wing.

The trip is extremely uneventful, apart from another service station faux-pas. A teacher admits to leaning over a group of students who are sitting down and saying "Oh I love chips" before stealing one of their fries. Again, not our students.

## 11. It wasn't a pen.

My office has a view out on to the road and the front gate of the school. It can be very useful when you are waiting for parents or students to arrive. I just happen to be looking out of the window at the same time as a scuffle is happening between a student and his Dad, turning up late to school for a meeting. The Dad punches him as the kid falls into the gate, fighting back. I was very alarmed at the force of the father towards his son, and was quite concerned for his welfare. My boss and I run down and my boss takes the student indoors to check him over and get him away from his abusive parent. Shit! It is the violent Dad and me. He starts telling me about how he is at the end of his tether, getting his son to attend school and he has no idea what to do. I really feel for him; I can understand that school puts a lot of pressure on parents with Fixed Penalty Notices, lawsuits, and even potential prison sentences, and this guy has just lost his shit. I understand his frustrations, but there is certainly a line there that he has crossed. I empathise with him, and encouragingly tell him to go home and wait for a call. God knows who from.

\*　　\*　　\*　　\*　　\*

A student in our room has handed me his iPad to help him with his work. He has failed to notice that when I go to get rid of the tabs on his internet pages they are mostly pornography. I hand him back his iPad and regret my choices in life.

\*　　\*　　\*　　\*　　\*

I have an urgent call to get a student out of a lesson. I'm not sure of what the urgency is, but this is often a physical altercation, so I rush there as fast as I can. I get down to his English classroom slightly out of breath, and the student is being restrained by his mates as an English teacher stands behind a few chairs, shouting at the top of his voice for the kid to get out. The student has punched him in the back of the head whilst he is at his computer. It is an awful situation, and I don't know who is in the wrong. And at this point, it doesn't matter. We have a responsibility to ensure both the teacher and the child feel protected and safe. Not only that, but this will get around the school like wildfire, so we need to try and settle the rest of the class as calmly as possible, before we have a riot on our hands.

We get the student to a quiet safe area as quickly as possible for him to calm down, as we find the underlying cause of this all. The teacher is visibly shaking and we feel it best for him to go and get a cup of tea. The student is collected by his parent and we don't see him again for two weeks until he comes in for a meeting with his Dad. The kid looks ill and we are quite concerned about him. After asking a few questions, we realise the student is actually fine, it's just that one of his friends at a party has shaved both his eyebrows off. During the meeting as we go through the options of what to do with the child, his father's phone starts ringing. The ring tone is one he has recorded himself. He is extremely nonplussed that the ringtone says "ANSWER THE PHONE YOU CUNT" on repeat.

Suddenly it all makes sense.

*****

We've got a student with us today, and he is just constantly talking. He is struggling with the work set for him, and these students tend to have a fear of failure, and can be very fatalistic. Despite the help and support, he's just not getting the idea. We have given him several warnings and he is becoming increasingly more annoying. We already know he is basically going to have to re-do the day again, which is causing us great distress, as we would much rather have some peace and quiet tomorrow.

During an argument about 'why learning modern languages is important', I notice he has one of those pens that have multiple colourful biros in it. The student is chewing on it and I ask him not to. You just know that it will split, and we will have a 'Sir, my pen exploded' situation next. How pens explode on children is beyond me. I have never in my entire life, had a pen 'explode' on me.

I sit back down at my desk and e-mail his head of year suggesting he does another day for his constant disruption, distraction, and refusal to follow our instructions. During this time, it has dawned on me that I have seen one of these golden pens before and I ask the student to hand it to me. After another 10-minute argument, the student hands me the pen that has been in his mouth all day.

I e-mail the head of year again to say that she may have a trickier call to make as the student has clearly been chewing on a vibrator all day. I'm quite concerned about where he has got this from. Thoughts are swimming around my head with worries of sexual exploitation, grooming, images, etc. As the head of year braces herself for the phone call, she's quite shocked by the mother's response. Turns out the child had been going through his Mum's drawers (not sure what for) and it was hers. The poor boy had no idea what he was actually chewing on. The mother does not seem that concerned, or embarrassed.

*　*　*　*　*

My lovely teacher girlfriend and I are going great guns. I am even thinking about moving in, engagements and having kids. This is the first time I've ever looked in to the future like this, and I'm absolutely bowled over. This is so positive. It is time to sort my life out properly, lose a bit of weight, and cut this drinking shit out.

\* \* \* \* \*

We have heard there is a big problem with our year 11's... drugs. Marijuana is being bought and sold in the school and is being used after school, on the green opposite. We know this as it has been reported to us by a picture on Snapchat from a staff member's daughter. We find the culprit and give him a full backpack and jacket search to no avail.

As I return him to his classroom, his friend next to him smells so badly of weed that it's easy to remove him from the room and find his scales and paraphernalia. He is sent home for the day and is suspended for two days before returning to school to sell once more. Clearly a good lesson learned.

\* \* \* \* \*

A kid has called me a cunt today and I am feeling slightly deflated. I love working with the naughty kids, as I can get on a level with them. When I'm the one they are falling out with, I feel like I've failed.

The woman I work with has had a couple of weeks off and it has been really hard work without her. I find out the reason is her dog has died and I am less than sympathetic about the two weeks off. When she returns to work, I can see in her eyes that two weeks was probably not long enough.

The drugs problem is getting worse and we hear of a student who is selling prescription medication to other students. We pull him in to the deputy head's office, search him, and find 20 individually wrapped Xanax tablets. He denies that he's dealing anything. They are removed from him and he goes back to his lessons. I asked the deputy head why he's been allowed back into lessons, who says that we have no evidence that he was dealing. I explain that he is definitely dealing drugs due to the individually wrapped tablets, but the deputy head says there is nothing we can do about it, as we haven't caught him red-handed and he hasn't admitted to it. I am gobsmacked. I suggest infiltrating the gang by wearing a backwards baseball cap and talking like a character from Top Boy.

\* \* \* \* \*

Another game of Saturday football and I'm refereeing the best I can. I've had to sub our star player as he is acting like an idiot and being quite abusive to the opposition and his own team. He is now refusing to leave the pitch. I'm fuming. I tell him we will just call the game off. He knows this is an empty threat as the other school has travelled 20 miles for a friendly. He eventually leaves the pitch, sits down and begins to abuse the opponent's manager who is also the linesman.

The linesman has asked me to get rid of the kid. I walk over and tell the kid to go back to the changing rooms, which he is obviously refusing. I tell him what the consequences of his actions will be. He removes his shirt and spits on it. He then turns and throws his shirt in my face before going back to the changing room and going home. I report this all to the SLT link of the PE department, the head of PE and the head of year. The student is banned from football for two weeks.

This ban lasts a week due to them having an important cup game.

> \* \* \* \* \*

We have had lockdown training just in case anything really awful happens like a weather warning, an active gunman or an apocalyptic war. The bell sounds in a certain way and we lock our doors and hide under our desks. The kids are seriously enjoying the drill, making fart noises, and crawling around. It is hard not to join in. We obviously never think we have to use this drill. We get a knock on the door from SLT and we start our lesson again with truly excited students.

Within the week, we have our first lock down. Wind has blown tiles off the roof and they are flying everywhere. We are in lock down whilst we wait for the area to be cordoned off. No one really knows what's going on and we all think it's a serious situation; the kids have got a feeling that something is going on too and there is a feel of unease in the lessons. Silence around the desks before SLT come along and tell us we can leave. Two hours later the head of drama has arrived at the pub after being missed by SLT and spending three hours in a costume cupboard with 30 silent students.

\* \* \* \* \*

Great news - the head is leaving! Well, great news for me. I had the feeling I really could not do well by him; I was just always going to get in to trouble. I'm just glad he is leaving before I was asked to go. If he were made of chocolate he would have definitely ate himself. I remember going to an assembly once and he was playing his guitar and singing to a group of dumbfounded year 11's. When Ofsted were in, he turned in to Ronald McDonald, doing keep ups on the field with 20 kids, despite not knowing one child's name. A real plastic tool bag.

\*     \*     \*     \*     \*

I've got a call for a student who is on top of a seven foot wall and is refusing to get down. As I get there, I know that this is going to be a pain in the arse, as I know that this kid is a pain in the arse. He's only been on trial here for a week or so. "Can you get down please?" I lead with this as obviously no-one has asked him this already. "No and you can't make me!" Now in all the training I have had, I have been taught that you can restrain a student if he is in danger of causing pain to himself, someone else, or his surroundings. I feel this kid is doing all three as he could damage the wall, the floor, himself and myself so I feel if I wanted to, I really could remove this kid from the wall. Therefore, my reply to him is, "I could get you down if I really have to, but I'd rather you came down on your own".

Damn. This kid has seen this as a threat and is going apeshit! He has just told me that he is going to stab me, which is a little harsh, and then he is going to get his Dad to come and beat me up. "How big is he?" I say to lighten the mood. The kid has seen this as another sign of aggression and I am now swimming uphill trying to deal with this angry foul-mouthed child. I tell him that I am the only one trying to help him so he should start trying to help himself. He is still walking away from me calling me every name he has learnt so far and has walked clean off-site; I report to the office that he has gone and go back to my office to ring home. I ring Mum over Dad just in case he is already on his way to school.

\* \* \* \* \*

I have gone out of bounds to use my vape pen. I have seen three students down the lane running in the opposite direction. I shout, but they are still running. At that point, one of the heads of year pulls up and asks me if I have seen these children. I jump in and we are in hot pursuit. We stop the three absconders and get them in the car to drive them back to school. Personally I'm not too sure of the right thing to do here, but the driver said he is insured, and he is higher up the hierarchy than me, so I'll leave him to it. On the way back, we ask the students what they were up to and they say they were just messing about. (They reek of cigarettes). I turn to the lads (obviously lads) and say, "you boys really smell of cigarettes". One of them tells us that they were standing by some sixth formers who were smoking.

"WE WERE SMOKING!" blurts out the middle student. I could see in the eyes of the other two lads that this is the last time they invite the student with Tourette's for a fag.

## 12. For whom the bell tolls.

The acting headteacher is the old head's best mate and he is almost as big an idiot but I quite like him, as he has always been nice to me. I ask him for some history work from his lesson as sadly one of the students in his class has been suspended. He said he would get right on it.

The next day I email him for the work again – no reply this time. He must be very busy.

I happen to bump into him in the staff room and say, "Oh, you haven't got that work, have you? I have to send that home today".

His face looks like I have asked him to clean my house with a toothbrush. "How DARE you bother me about this again! I will do this when I am ready to do this. QUIT bothering me about this work." He might as well have just said "I AM AN IMPORTANT MAN" and started beating his chest like Tarzan. I wait for another two days for work for this excluded child to never arrive and then send a worksheet about Tudors at a year 7 level to a GCSE student.

\* \* \* \* \*

It's Summer time and the clocks haven't changed correctly in school. Due to this, the bells are going off at the wrong time of the day. I don't think too much of this; we all know what the time is, and can figure out what's gone wrong here. As it's quite quiet in the behaviour room today, I pop into some classes to check in on some of the more difficult characters in our school, and make sure they are managing well in their lessons. I attempt to go into an English classroom, but the door isn't budging. Strangely, the lights are off too. I give the door a nudge, and it's definitely not locked, but something is pushed up against it. I call out to the teacher, and put the lights on. A cabinet has been pushed up against the door, and I spot the students and teachers all hidden underneath their desks. Turns out the teacher thought the bell was another lockdown, and they've been hiding under their desks for the last 20 minutes.

\*    \*    \*    \*    \*

A student in year 10 is pregnant. It has got around the staff pretty quickly as the mother has rang in to complain about the standard of the sex education at the school.

\*    \*    \*    \*    \*

I have a call to help a music lesson where it is "all kicking off!". I arrive to see several students outside the class, not willing to enter the room. The room is a large hexagonal building with high ceilings and cupboards full of instruments all along one side. As I go in, students have set up two barricades either side of the room and are throwing xylophone beaters at each other (it looks like a lot of fun). I enter the room screaming, so I don't get hit with any beaters and to also make these kids stop. I shout about respecting school equipment and the consequences to their behaviour. As I go to leave the room all the boys involved are stunned into a bit of silence.

One of the cupboards slowly opens and a young man's head pops out about eight foot off the ground on one of the shelves. "Has he gone?"

\* \* \* \* \*

We have an end of year charity football match set up between the sixth formers and the staff. The staff have some 'alright-ish' players, but the majority are just pretty fit and up for a laugh. We get quite a bit of a crowd, a good few hundred kids lining the banks of the 3G pitch; the game is played in good spirits (the majority of the time). The sixth formers have made their own kit with a sponsorship of "Brazzers"; they have written their nicknames on the back and they have set up their own Twitter feed. They've even got polls and 'Match of the Day'-style line-up videos; it's all in really good fun. They've even set up a DJ who then becomes commentator, who then becomes suspended after saying the staff member right-back looked like a paedophile, across the microphone. Unfortunately, for me, being massively overweight and having to try a lot harder to keep up, I began to take the game a little too seriously. I am slightly late into a tackle and get a warning from the year 10 referee. With a couple of minutes to go, the sixth formers are awarded an incredibly soft penalty and the young referee thinks that this is hilarious. I feel that as this is a friendly and for charity, it is a massive injustice (hindsight is a wonderful thing; I was so pathetic). I pick the ball up off the penalty spot and kick it as far as I can over the fence into the empty field. The referee books me. With everything I have done in my life I genuinely think that this is one of the most shameful. We lose 2-1.

\* \* \* \* \*

One of the most annoying things about my job is that sometimes you are called upon to deal with students at lunch or break time. Today is one of those days and I've been called to deal with a student on the playground. As I arrive, it is an ex-student; an ex-student who has been expelled a few weeks earlier for being an idiot in general. As I approach, I can see clearly that he is in an awful get-up. Dirty trainers, ripped jeans, an unsightly hoodie and a leather jacket over the top of it. I think he is holding a weapon, which instantly triggers me in to panic. On closer inspection, it is a half-full bottle of Budweiser (he is 14). "What are you doing here Tony?", I ask this total idiot. "Someone owes me money, don't they". It seems that in his three weeks outside of school, his accent suggests that he has joined the So Solid Crew. I cannot hold my laughter as he swigs from the bottle, noticeably wincing. I remove him from school site and ask him not to return. When escorting him off the school site, from the smell of him, I can tell he does not want any police involvement.

* * * * *

A student who has to spend the whole day with me has arrived late and is incredibly tired, with bloodshot eyes and is struggling to get a full sentence together. He slowly eats a multi-pack size of Doritos and is giggling about things he remembers. He stinks of weed. I cannot find anyone to get to my office so we can search his bag (you have to have a witness if you are to search a child's bag, for safeguarding reasons). I feel that whilst we are one to one, I should probably talk candidly to him about his drug usage and how it could be detrimental to his life and his future.

He tells me that I haven't got any proof that he has been smoking weed (even though he is looking like a person in a cartoon, if you were told to draw someone who smokes a lot of weed). I tell him he stinks of weed! He says "PROVE IT".

One nil to him! He is right. I cannot prove anything and with a conversation, he has ran out of the room, to come back another day. He has taught me a very valuable lesson; don't bother questioning or accusing a child before you have the evidence.

**13 8 minus pen equals 3.**

We have had a call from a house down the road and I have arrived on their driveway to see a few students jump over a fence and back on to the school site. I knock on the door to the people who contacted us and they invite me in for a cup of tea. Never say no to a cup of tea when you work in a school, as you have no idea when the next one might be. On arrival in their very lovely kitchen, where they tell me about the problems of the youth of today, I notice on their mini whiteboard on their wall, they have in quite large writing, the phone number to my office. I ask them how they got the number and they say it was given to them by the old headteacher. I finish my tea and apologise for everything every student from my school has ever done. On the way out, I manage to just about using my index finger to turn the eight in our phone number to a three.

\* \* \* \* \*

We have broken up. I got a call from her on a Sunday night to say that she does not think that it is working out. My world collapses and I immediately turn back to booze. Oh shit, I did not even think about this. I have to go back to my crap job and see her tomorrow. This is going to be a long few terms. Every day I obviously have to see her around the corridors and my heart breaks every time I see her. I think about leaving. However, I feel like I have put too much work in since my warning (which lasts twelve months) to just go somewhere else. In addition, I would look so pathetic, even though I am dying inside. I just get on with my job with my head down, crying most evenings and drinking as much as I can until I sleep.

\* \* \* \* \*

I am waiting to take an extra-curricular football training (I felt that perhaps throwing myself into something to keep my mind busy is the best option), and a man is standing opposite me in the corridor in a tracksuit, holding football boots in his hands. He asks me if I work here and then asks me about football and my experiences. I tell him all about the local reserves team I help to run, what level I have played at, who I have had trials for back in the day, and how my Sunday team is getting on... I've been talking non-stop for about ten minutes.

I say to him "What about yourself?" suspecting him to be a Dad of one the students.

"Oh, I'm Stuart Slater, I'm running your session today!"

"As in Watford... Ipswich, Stuart Slater?" I reply.

"Yeah" he says, extra casually.

"I'm really sorry for boring you," I say sheepishly.

"Thanks".

I go in to the changing rooms to tell the kids to hurry the FUCK up.

*　　*　　*　　*　　*

We have an amazing SEN department at this school; we have quite a few students who suffer with autism, Asperger's Syndrome, or something of that nature. They are all amazing students and it's fantastic to see them being integrated into school life, building relationships with students and staff alike.

Having said that, you do sometimes get a little wobble here and there.

One of the students who has a lot of SEN needs, has been in the toilet for quite a long time and some older boys have taken this opportunity to pour three bottles of water over the top of his cubicle. The students know he loves a good long poo, and he's quite often in the toilets for well over half an hour. His head of year has had many conversations with his parents in regards to his particularly unhealthy diet, which leads him to needing the toilet quite regularly, but to add to this, our suspicion is that he is just so much happier by himself, when he doesn't have to learn, work, or socialise with staff or students. In this instance, he has quite understandably hit the roof. He is now on an all-out rampage and I, being first on the scene, will have to sort this out. When I arrive, he has destroyed the sports area. Every single piece of equipment has been trashed. Six 6-a-side goalposts are on the floor. Two tennis nets have been pulled out and eight netball posts are on the floor. He has also tipped a large amount of tennis balls on to the playground. It appears like a hurricane has swept through the sports area.

Hurricane Harris is a nickname that stays with this student up until he leaves in year 11.

*   *   *   *   *

We have a PTFA night where we try and raise money for things we desperately need at school; to do this, they invite the teachers along to spend their money earned from the school to help buy equipment they desperately need to teach their classes effectively (it makes perfect sense). This time it is a race night. I have drank, again probably a little too much for a school event. I feel de ja vu coming on. I forget that not every social activity involves getting as drunk as you can. The night goes alright and a lot better than the previous quiz night. At the end of the night, being the person I am, I decide to help out putting the chairs and tables away. All that is left is my friends' chair with his coat on it, and the chair of one of the mothers' on the other table, with her coat on it. On my way to look for him I unfortunately spot him in a maths classroom busying himself with her. I cough loudly and break it up as I am getting a lift home with him. He seems very pleased with himself. I really hope the student of the Mum finds out.

## 14. Shots fired... and consumed.

We have a new head! Everyone is incredibly excited and hopefully this will break up the boys club that we currently have here. You can tell which interviewee is going to get the job under the old head, as it is normally the best looking female.

She has arrived, stating that she is going to shake things up. Good on her. I wish her the best of luck, and as long as it is improving the school I love, then great. She is under five foot and has a real bulldog-chewing-a-wasp face. You can tell she is not going to take any shit from the kids. I think this is great. A fresh start; a new beginning.

\* \* \* \* \*

I get a call from a teacher to tell me that a student is acting strangely in her lesson. I collect the student and realise straight away that he is absolutely smashed. Really, truly hammered. He has stolen a bottle from his brothers' 'stash' and without a mixer, or any sense, has drunken two thirds of a litre bottle at lunch and can just about stand up. We ring the parents and get him collected. The highlight of the incident is when the deputy head asks him directly if he has been drinking and he replies, "I may have had a couple of shots" and then falls off his chair.

\* \* \* \* \*

Its school musical time! I have decided to broaden my horizons and help. I have spoken to the drama teacher and she has asked me to choreograph a dance routine. Now this could be interesting; the main reason I have taken this job on is that I quite fancy one of the music teachers. The musical is called "Honk" and those of you that do not know, it is the musical adaptation of The Ugly Duckling. It is not bad and the kids are very enthusiastic about it. The song I've been directed to choreograph is called "The Goose March", and involves about 15 kids who are in an army-style group of flying geese (if you pinch your thumb and index finger together on both hands then touch them at the tips together and then turn them upside down to go over your eyes you'll know what I mean). I have watched a lot of YouTube versions and settled on what I feel would be the best dance suited to our kids. It's in an army formation so certain students have to be on certain marks at the right time. It actually looked alright when it came to the first night of the performance.

On the second night, one student was off sick and they needed someone who knew the routine. Trying to impress the young music teacher, I did the gallant thing and stepped in. A 27-year-old borderline alcoholic, dressed as an army goose in V formation, in a child's outfit for the joy of 200 parents and staff. I decided to not get involved again – there's only so much you have to do in order to impress a woman.

\* \* \* \* \*

I must have impressed on the Devon activity trips, as I have been invited to attend an international trip. We are off to Belgium by coach, to see some battlefields and war trenches. I think this is because I like a laugh and a bit of a drink. The deputy head certainly has a similar mindset. It's an early start (3am) and I seem to be the only person, student or staff, that has all my stuff in a holdall. We are only staying for two nights?! The kids are boisterous on the coach (as always) and I am handed an envelope on the coach with "breakfast" scrawled on it. Inside is a £10 note. I think to myself that I could probably spend it on Toblerone. As I ask the ex-army science teacher how much breakfast on the ferry is, he tells me that the trip can go well or badly for me depending on whether I buy breakfast or Stella on the ferry with that £10. Three pints in an hour and 15 minutes is not easy on the bladder, but six episodes of Blackadder on the drive from Calais to Ypres helps to pass the time.

The trip is a real revelation; I would really recommend going to Ypres to anyone. I have never been interested in World War I or what happened, but now I love it. I have bought documentaries and books and sent my whole family to the same place; they have all come back raving about it. The staff on our trip really know their stuff and the driver is fantastic, giving tours as he navigates the windy-cobbled streets. Day one is the Flanders Field museum and well-renowned chocolate shop. My friend has given me a fake 50 Euro note that I spend in the market on a bratwurst.

Day two we are visiting trenches and cemeteries. It is absolutely amazing; I never realised the real scale of the atrocities. Millions died. Millions. Going to a graveyard that is not local, with only about 50 or 60 headstones in it is unreal. It is so well preserved and looked after; a real tearjerker. The English teacher on the trip is semi sensible and has a European surname. At each graveyard, there is a book with every name and details of who is buried there. The English teacher is annoyed that he is yet to find his name in any of the sites. I suggest he is looking at the wrong team sheet. He gets annoyed but then shuts up when we reach the German cemetery and he finds 20 soldiers with the same spelling.

The Menin Gate ceremony on the final day was a particularly humbling experience. We encouraged the children to write their own comments on the wreath, and we chose some trustworthy and reliable students to walk through the Menin Gate during the ceremony, to pay their respects by leaving their wreath at the altars. Times like this make you so incredibly proud of the little humans you are slowly building to become adults. We were lucky to have a pretty good trumpeter on this trip, and he played the bugle call for us at other cemeteries too.

In the evenings on trips, you have a little bit of free time where you normally sit around and talk about any issues and plan for the next day. On this particular trip, there's a football pitch outside, and after the very humbling and tear-jerking days, it's good to get out and play on the field. Once we've worn them down as much as possible, the aim is to get the students totally exhausted so that they are well behaved and in silence in their rooms. This is not just for them to get a good night's sleep, but also for us to have a bit of peace and quiet to crack open the port and cheese we've bought from the market. These sometimes get a little boozy and one night, a student comes down to the staff area to ask us to stop making so much noise, which is a little embarrassing.

Normally on the first night of a trip, you sit in corridors to make sure kids are not messing about or running in to each other's rooms, shouting and screaming. You do this until about midnight or one-o-clock, depending on the kids and the type of trip. About 11:45pm, six kids have come sprinting out of their room screaming at the top of their lungs. The ex-army science teacher and I are on duty; we hot-foot it to their room to tell the kids to be quiet and get back in their room, as they are disrupting the whole hostel (hostels in Belgium are particularly strict; if they break the noise regulations, there are fines to pay!)

Now, it is good to have a successful trip with kids, as it looks great on the school. If a hostel or member of the public e-mails your school to say how great you are, the headteacher normally jumps on this to praise everyone and you can hold your head high for a little while. Having said that, do not fall for it every time when a member of the public asks you what school you are from. Have a good look around first to see which kid has been a little shit, or if the member of public is smiling.

Going back to the story. These kids are making a racket, so we calm them down until they are making sense. There is a massive spider in their room, and they have all come running out. Ex-army dude and I are telling them not to be so stupid and to get back to bed, rolling our eyes at their childish manner, and in a show of good faith, we suggest we will remove the spider. He goes in first, with me following behind.

As we get into the room, I am knocked down by the ex-army guy bolting out, and in the middle of the floor, the biggest spider I have ever seen in my life. This thing had knees! Knees and a billion eyes, I would not have been surprised if Harry Potter came in after me to kill it. As we both run for the door, we get trapped in the door frame in our haste; it's like a Laurel and Hardy skit.

In the end, one of the kids was brave enough to remove it and we all got on with our lives. When I say get on with our lives, I sleep that night in tracksuit bottoms with football socks over the top and a hoodie tucked in with the hood tied closed. And a good amount of port to help me sleep.

## 15. Pornsnub

The new head seems okay, but the kids are constantly telling me how horrible she is. A real shouter. I think this is good for me, as hopefully there will be less incidents to deal with. Believe me, this can only be a good thing. The last head just didn't know how to be strict, and wanted to be every child's 'friend'. This is why the behaviour was becoming quite unruly.

I have received a call from a classroom to collect a student. When I arrive there, the student is outside the room trying to get back in. Luckily, it is the ex-army science teacher talking to him, so I know that this situation will get better. It doesn't. Myself and the other teacher are standing in the doorway whilst a student puts his head down and runs at us full pelt whilst screaming "GIVE ME MY FUCKING BAG!". We are more than willing to give him his bag, but not in the current state he is in.

As he hits us, he deflects off both of us to the floor and we do our best to avoid laughing at him. He storms off, sobbing. We feel bad for what has happened but we do have a good laugh about it down the pub.

\* \* \* \* \*

My impressive goose-dancing has wooed the music teacher and we have started dating. This can only go well but I have to do my best not to mess this up or be overly keen. I could not handle another 'break up and work with' situation. A lengthy Facebook messenger conversation has turned in to a bit of a kiss at work before school. Feeling great!

\* \* \* \* \*

A couple of students have had a bit of a brawl, and we have one of them with us, calming down. He is visibly shaking and clearly has no idea what he is doing. We leave him to cool off a bit, but we are letting him know that he is in a safe space and that we will talk to him when he has calmed down. After a while and a destroyed exercise book, he is beginning to open up about his problems. His Mum was in an adult movie. A full on hard-core pornographic movie and somehow the other lad has found out and they are fighting, as it is now common knowledge. He's understandably mortified and angry with the way that they are speaking about his Mum. We have no idea how to deal with this as a school and have decided the best way to tackle it is head on; bring in Mum for a meeting. A week later, she is on her way in to school and from my office, I am thinking how awkward this meeting is going to be. I also think about how many hours I've wasted googling this woman. I am relieved I could not find the evidence.

\*     \*     \*     \*     \*

There has been a drama trip to the play 'Woman in Black' over the weekend. The drama teachers have seen this play over and over again, and they feel like playing a trick on the students. On the coach-ride there they 'whisper' (loudly enough for the students to hear), talking about 'what happened last time'. When the student's become curious and ask for the story, the drama teacher explains that last time, something crawled over their heads and came through the ceiling on one of their laps. The students are understandably nervous, and as the play becomes more and more creepy, the drama teachers give each other a nod, and start their 'acting'. They look up a few times, ask to switch seats with a student here and there, and a few sweets are thrown into students' laps, making them scream at unsuitable times. Clearly this has become a little too much for one student, who just wants everyone to be safe. At one point in the play, the killer is on the loose and a woman gets out of the car to see what's happening, but not knowing the killer is there... one of our students has shouted "DON'T GET OUT THE CAR!". The teacher's sink into their seats, heads down, with an aim not to be seen by the audience who by this time, have had quite enough of their distractions.

\* \* \* \* \*

We have visitors in the school from Kazakhstan. In our morning briefing, the headteacher has asked the staff to try to stop the students from doing Borat impressions. One of the PE staff shouts "but why?" in a faultless Borat voice. It is the biggest laugh we have had in one of these meetings. The headteacher looked totally unimpressed. There was likely a telling-off at some point for that one. I'm just glad they blurted it out before I did.

\* \* \* \* \*

We have an at 80-year-old helper in DT and he is a legend. Staff and students all love him. He's ex-navy and he is one of the nicest people I have ever met. He is excellent at his job and great to be around, a dab hand at anything and always willing to help you out. Luckily for me, he is an Arsenal fan, so we have lots to talk about and I love hearing his old stories of the Highbury days. He has booked a cruise for his wedding anniversary and wants a day off school.

The head has denied the day off and he has quit. The whole school is devastated. Questions are being asked and apparently, the head would not budge to give him one day off from his part-time job for his 50th wedding anniversary.

It's beginning to look like it's not only the kids who hate this new head. She lost a lot of friends that day. I hope she learned a lesson from that.

\*   \*   \*   \*   \*

A job has come up for a head of house. The house system is really good and looks like a lot of fun. It's all about building the community of the school vertically so that the younger years get to know the older years, and provide a sense of competition too. The school is separated in to four colours and named after four different scientists. The house assemblies are pretty dull; I feel I can give this system the kick up the bum it so sorely needs.

The interview starts poorly as it is a three-part process. Meeting with staff, meeting with kids and then a written task. My chances are bolstered however, as I am the only one who has applied.

The interview with the kids goes well (as I knew it rather would) but then the interview with staff is horrific and I am far too relaxed; I make a huge pig's ear of it. At one point I think standing up and walking out would be a better use of everyone's time. They ask me about the 'community feel' of the house system and I start talking about the local shop and how we could help people out in the community which overall is a really stupid idea, and I've clearly got the wrong end of the stick.

I didn't get the job.

This is really embarrassing as the position remains unfilled. They genuinely think that no one doing this job would be better than me doing it. Ouch!

Sadly, they are probably right... nothing the pub cannot solve.

\*     \*     \*     \*     \*

It is coming up to the end of the year, and the sixth form have their leaving day. This is slightly earlier than everyone else due to their A Level exams. On their last day they normally arrange a theme, plan a good fancy dress and pull the occasional prank. This year they have decided to have a go at the new head and say in poster form that they preferred the old head. There are "WANTED" signs all around the school with her face on it. It's quite funny and meant in a good spirit and a very normal thing for our students to do such a thing. A good roast by the sixth form is always in good spirits and not really meant to offend.

The headteacher has been seen crying and we are now going around removing the pictures.

The head has cancelled her speech at the sixth form leaving assembly.

The head has now cancelled the sixth form Leaver's Ball. With students spending money on transport, dresses, and all that vodka hidden in water bottles.

This has set a dangerous precedent and is a little too precious for my liking.

## 16. Fairygate

A head of year has caught a student squashing a sandwich on the outside of a window and is really not best pleased about it. The student has been told that he has to clean it up himself and the head of year has brought along a sponge and a bucket of water for him, but the student is refusing to clean it off. When the head of year returns to our office, we are informed that the student will be spending a few days in our main room and she is off to the car to dry off and calm down a little. Turns out that the shouting match, with parent and teacher vs. student, leads to him pouring the entire bucket right over the head of year's head.

\* \* \* \* \*

I get a call to attend a languages lesson for a student who is flat out refusing to play ball and has been asked to leave. By the time I get there, he is running around the room thinking he is hilarious and distracting the rest of the class. I tell him to wait outside and I wait in the doorway for him to go past me, so I can tell the class about the high expectations we have at our school. Whilst doing this, the boy who has been removed has slammed the door with my hand in it, leaning against the frame. I turn on my heels and start running at the boy and he has started to leg it down the corridor. I give chase for about ten metres or so before deciding that today isn't the best day to lose my job as I have a mates stag do coming up. I just continue running until I'm outside of school and let off some steam (go for a vape).

\* \* \* \* \*

A student has run away and this time he means it! He is not stopping. Luckily down the end of the corridor I see him slip into an empty classroom. By the time I get there he spots me coming in and takes a running jump at the open window. Sadly for this poor boy, this window, albeit very clean, is not open. He smashes through the window and lands in a heap on the other side. The window smashes into hundreds of thousands of tiny little squares and after a couple of seconds of looking at the carnage, he is off again. I think it's probably best to leave him like you would a bolted horse, and I begin to clean the glass off the teachers table and call the site team.

Later on CCTV, we all have a good watch and contemplate the money if we sent this in to Harry Hill.

\*   \*   \*   \*   \*

The head's PA and I mutually do not get along. I think she is possibly the rudest woman I've ever met in my life and I'm sure that she thinks the same of me. The only time we ever have to speak is when she wants some work to be sent home for an excluded student, and she adds the letter from the head about their reintegration back into school. Today the PA has decided that she is going to up the rudeness-factor and has come into my office. Without speaking, she has thrown the empty envelope at my desk and turned on her heels to go back to her incredibly important 12 grand-a-year job. Normally, I would take this on the chin; today however, I've had enough. I pick up the envelope and start my walk to her office.

I weigh up the pros and cons of what I want to do and what I'm going to do. My heart wins on this occasion. I open up her door to her office and I throw the envelope back on her desk and walk away. As I saunter off, I regret my choices, and await the phone call.

Lo and behold, a call from the head follows and I am told about how unprofessional I am. I disagree with her and she begins to raise her voice at me. "Do you mind not shouting at me?". "I will shout at whoever the hell I want, because I'm a headteacher!". "Well I'm a human being and I won't be shouted at, and I won't have things thrown at me". She gives me a verbal warning and I feel like a naughty kid again. I'm still not sure how I was in the wrong here; I think my face doesn't fit with her.

\* \* \* \* \*

It's coming up to the end of the academic year and sadly a few staff who I get on really well with are leaving. My office usually gets used by the heads' PA to hide the gifts for staff (wine, sometimes flowers). The heads' PA then passes the head the gifts when she provides a leaving speech for each staff member. As a good mate is leaving to work in a mobile kitchen unit, going to festivals and so forth, I change his bottle of wine for the bottle of Fairy liquid that is in the staffroom kitchen. Not my best joke, but one I will find fairly amusing if he notices the bottle of washing up liquid during his speech, or someone else's, whilst he has to be quiet. I stash the bottle of wine with all the other gifts, with a plan to give it to him later when I confess that it was me.

About an hour later I go to his classroom and ask him if he likes his present. He pulls out a bottle of wine and tells me he doesn't particularly like wine. I'm confused but think nothing of it.

When I return to my office, Miss Marple and Jessica Fletcher (The head and her PA), are there and all hell has broken loose. They start by accusing me of trying to steal the bottle of wine. They continue with this line of questioning until I end up receiving a written warning. No matter how much I say it was just a joke and they need to lighten up, as I hand them back the wine, they didn't find it too funny.

"Do you want the teacher to think that I, the headteacher of this school, thought it would be appropriate to buy him some washing up liquid as a gift?".

At that point I understood. It wasn't about the theft of a bottle of wine; it wasn't about the staff member having a gift taken from him. It was about her. How she might be perceived; at no point did I think about that, because it wasn't meant like that. I had no idea just how much she cared about what people thought of her and how much she needed to be the 'top dog'. I'm angry. Not upset, not even sorry. Just angry.

* * * * *

Sports day today! It's been a great day with zero rain which is really unusual. The SLT (in their infinite wisdom) have given the students poster paint to use as face paint in the afternoon. The kids are absolutely covered. The yellow house looks like Minions who wished to be big.

With all these kids covered in paint, one class has decided to get in the school spirit, and colour their teachers coat yellow. In particular, his rather smart suit jacket, innocently left on his chair, while he was in the staff room at lunch. As you may have realised after this, no paint is allowed at all future sports days. Well done SLT. Good call.

## 17. Anglo-Italian relations

A boy has come to us with poo on his blazer. He's extremely ashamed and I've taken his uniform down to PE to be cleaned and dried before he goes home. I've asked him what has happened and after a while he's embarrassedly told me. He was going for a poo at the same time as his mate next door in the cubicles. He thinks it would be funny to poo on to a tissue and throw it over the top at his mate. I find this bit quite funny, although a little bit disgusting. Sadly (for him and not for this book) his throw didn't quite make it over the top and has deflected off his cubicle and back on to his head and blazer. A lot of the time you don't need teachers to teach valuable lessons.

\* \* \* \* \*

I've been invited on a rugby tour abroad and without ever having thrown a rugby ball in my life, I'm quite excited about the trip to Milan. I've been there with a previous girlfriend and I know my way around. We will be competing in three games and plenty of training sessions. The hotel has one star on the Trip Advisor reviews across the board and I'm expecting something similar to where Jesus was born. Which will come in really handy if our driver doesn't know the directions. "Follow the star, mate" as I get on the coach from the airport. He was definitely Italian, and had no idea what I was on about.

The hotel is in the middle of nowhere, and visits to the 'local' cities of Venice and Milan take 2-3 hours each. The weather is torrential and I'm running out of dry clothes, stupidly thinking I can wear the same pair of shorts twice. This is not the Italy I remember.

The first game should have been called off. As I walk across the field, the pitch is coming up to my shins in water and mud. Quite an uneventful game initially, ends with me travelling to a hospital with a student who has had his hand stamped on by an opposing player. It is always a difficult situation when going to a foreign hospital and having very little grasp of the language. In an Italian hospital (in my one experience), a person is put in a wheelchair immediately, so it is easier to manoeuvre the patient around. On our way down a long corridor we are parked next to a door. The door is opened by a nurse leaving a room and left open. Inside... a dead woman. The woman is lying in state position and at the stage in a movie before the blanket is pulled up over the face. The kid isn't too happy about it and I push him several feet down the corridor. We speak about life.

The male nurse is a very happy soul and asks said student to clench his fist and raise his arm across his chest to his left shoulder.

"For Italia!" he says before playfully slapping our student around the face and laughing very loudly. He's enjoyed slapping an Englishman today. I am a little shocked!

After a couple of hours, the student is strapped up and we return to the venue of the first ever underwater rugby match, in which our little school has beaten a fairly respected rugby club in Milan.

As we are chatting after the match, the host asks us if we would like a "stronger drink". The teacher in charge has asked if they have any wine and the option of red or white is offered. We choose red and 30 minutes later, the host arrives back with a bottle of red. We are then told that he has gone home to get it. We are very gracious, but his wine is pretty much undrinkable.

On our table, the manager of the other side is arguing with the referee of our game quite loudly in Italian, and it has caught the attention of everyone in the room. This leads to an almighty headbutt to the manager square on the nose and punches begin flying over our table; we are hoping he knocks the wine over. The fight spills out to the stairwell (the only exit) and the kids are looking quite scared.

"Can we leave, Sir?"

"What, through the fight?" my partner asks, trying to spot an easier exit. We gallantly step in, cool the situation, and swiftly get our kids out of there.

The next day we have a day off of sorts. That is, no training, no fixtures. Instead, we have to make entertainment for the children in the hostel, as the rain is stopping them from running around outside. We have planned a quiz in the evening; me being me, I have offered to present it.

We speak to the lovely reception lady and she has told us that there is a 'festival' up the road. My colleague and I are sent up the road in the rain to check the place out. We are hoping it's somewhere we can entertain the students for a while.

It is a five mile trek and we arrive drenched, already deciding that after the festival we plan to get a taxi home. We arrive in a beautiful Italian village with an impressive clocktower and a beautiful square. We can't find a festival, so we decide to have a coffee and warm up before finding a taxi to return back. We ask the waiter where the festival is and he points us in the direction through a tunnel. We have our coffees and start making our way to the festival, already knowing that walking 25 year 11's and sixth formers five miles in the rain is not going to do anybody any favours.

The festival... wow. We pay 20 Euros each and we are given a lanyard and a wine glass that fits in to the pouch in the lanyard. We are told in extremely rough English that we are to sample the wine from the different vineyards and mark each one out of ten, ready for the grand winner to be announced the next day. There are twenty different wines to sample and no shot glasses here. We are having our second wine and a bit of a chat, before we decide to check in with the trip leader. We tell him about the journey and that we will get a cab home, but we have only really just got here. After our sixth full glass of red wine (I think they are giving us more to hopefully mark them up on our scoresheets) we haven't marked one under an 8 yet and we are having a lovely time of it. Glass nine and my friend is third in the queue in a conga and I've jumped in as well (to obviously build Anglo-Italian relations). Glass 14 is our first wine we've rated a seven, and glass 16 is now being balanced on my head as we try to get to 17.

We can't find a cab, so we take a couple of beers from a nearby shop for our walk home. All that festival-going has made us thirsty.

We get back to the hotel and the trip leader is standing there, with (how my mind remembers it) a rolling pin like Andy Capp's wife.

"So, is the festival appropriate for the kids?"

Do you know what... I've never laughed more in my life.

PS. The quiz goes badly, and my mate accidentally calls a kid a "fucking idiot".

## 18. "Chapter 1"

I have been called to the heads' office and I have the feeling where your stomach just drops. I feel sick and I have no idea what I'm going in for. It could be a big deal, or it could be a huge deal. It's never normally a good deal. The head makes you feel like you are nothing but an inconvenience to her. I have never been told well done, or good job. I know that I'm doing a good job because the kids are improving. I dread these unplanned meetings. I go and ask the heads' PA what the meeting is about, and she can't tell me. I wander around the school, continuously worried. I go and make myself sick, so I hopefully feel better, but now I'm just worried with the taste of sick in my throat and watering eyes. I can't cope with this. I should just walk out and keep going. I lie to myself and say to myself that it may be for a good reason. I know full well it won't be. I have a little cry as I can't cope with the anguish. I start thinking about everything it could be. With this head it could be anything... literally anything.

The meeting is pushed back because they are busy.

I walk into the heads' office and a piece of paper is put in front of me with a comment I made on Facebook. It's a fictitious quote from a kid; I think it may have been from Arrested Development or Curb Your Enthusiasm.

I'm asked by the head why I wrote this on Facebook, "a public forum". I explain that it's from a TV show and she doesn't believe me; she gives me a proper dressing down about bringing the schools name into disrepute. I ask who gave her the printout and she says she cannot tell me. I tell her that the sad thing is that my privacy settings are very high and it must be from one of the eight staff I'm friends with at the school.

Another verbal warning and the feeling of worthlessness.

\*   \*   \*   \*   \*

On my way into work and I contemplate just driving into a tree, so I don't have to work. Nothing major, but it would be a couple of days in hospital which would be better than working.

I think about this a lot. Throwing myself down some stairs is the main one. Just a few days off is all I need.

\*   \*   \*   \*   \*

It is parent's day at school again. This time I am prepared. I have brought snacks and borrowed my mates' Netflix password. Cannot wait until 4pm.

\* \* \* \* \*

It's the end of the academic year and we are having a Saturday evening leaving do as three major long-term staff members are leaving. Everyone quietly knows they are leaving due to our new head. The evening starts around 7pm and we have all brought our own booze. I've bought 24 cans of Carling and I am willing to share.

The head of drama has started her speech and she has written a story about her husband, who is leaving. She starts with "Chapter One" and it's all done in good taste; it's getting a good laugh from people who like that sort of thing.

At 9-o-clock she is on to chapter 19 and the DJ has set up, twiddling his thumbs. Some people have already left, making their excuses. I'm about twelve cans deep now and wish I'd brought spirits.

Roughly 9.30pm; her self-indulgent rant ends, and we are all sent home.

\*  \*  \*  \*  \*

Our head is off work and there is a much more relaxed feeling around the staff; people are smiling again. A science teacher tells us a funny story but it's actually horrifically sad if you think about it. She went to see the head and asked her how she could progress through the school as she's been doing really well in her department, as well as doing a lot of extra-curricular. The head replied, sitting back in her chair, with, "So, whose job do you want then? You're obviously after someone's job... whose is it?" The science teacher then tells us that she subsequently handed in her notice, and has got a promotion at another school.

* * * * *

I'm always friends with the PE department. I'm a keen sportsman and love to get involved, and they are always very appreciative of a staff member who doesn't mind taking up their evenings and Saturday's with training or fixtures. When they get a new member of staff, I always make sure they feel welcome, as I know they will eventually be my mate and this has never not worked; they are always nice people. This one will be more difficult as he is a Spurs fan. We get on extremely well, but today I've upset him. A kid was struggling in the pool and he has used the life-saving pole to help the student to the edge of the swimming pool. This kid is splashing about so much that he has grabbed the pole and pulled my mate right in. I am absolutely pissing myself laughing, but he is yet to see the funny side of it. It has also been a mistake uploading this incident to Facebook so I can remember the anniversary in years to come.

\*   \*   \*   \*   \*

The students at our school are showing how tolerant they can be of other peoples' cultures and religions by singing the "One Pound Fish" song at our one Indian teacher.

\*   \*   \*   \*   \*

It's prom night and this is going to be a good one. The head 'unfortunately cannot be there' and everyone has let their guard down a bit and is really enjoying themselves. There are more staff on the dance floor than students and it is a great night. One student has had a rucksack confiscated full of booze. He has literally just taken what he can from his parents drinks cabinet, including a crystal decanter of whisky, along with a bottle of Advocaat. I've called home to get him picked up and his parents are incredibly ashamed. I've offered whether they would like me to deliver the alcohol to them. They are suitably embarrassed and have asked for all the alcohol to be destroyed.

That we do...

The party continues back at a PE teachers' house, long in to the night.

\*     \*     \*     \*     \*

The heads PA has bought a card for every tutor group (that's 42 cards), and every child is instructed to sign it, so that it can be sent to the head in hospital. We find out that her operation is a cosmetic one and not actually life-saving; a lot of staff refuse to sign the cards.

I don't agree with any of this. The instruction that students must send their regards, to somebody they don't respect? For staff to sign a card, just so that theyheadteacher feels cared about? Only in recent months, a teacher has had a serious operation for cancer, as well as chemotherapy, radiotherapy, and a really tough time along with it. Not even a thought of a card or flowers from the school.

## 19. Frankfart

I've been asked to give an assembly on bullying. It goes really well and I'm quite proud of it. It has some audience participation too. I once went on a tour of Wembley Stadium and saw the tour guide do this. I asked for a student to come up and bully me; some students like doing it, some are a little shyer. I ask them to point to the ceiling and then I hang my jacket on their finger pointing at the ceiling, covering their face.

It goes down really well for the first three assemblies. Because it is doing well, the head has come to see it.

I am subsequently brought to her office and told how inappropriate the assembly was. A good number of kids say it's the best assembly they've seen.

\* \* \* \* \*

It's my 30th birthday. I spend the evening sitting in the school hall at a presentation evening. All the awards go to good kids, so I pretty much only recognise the ones who play football.

\* \* \* \* \*

There is a maths trip to Frankfurt. A tour of an Audi museum, a walk around the zoo, a tour of the stock exchange and the highlight, a walking tour of the financial district. I have zero interest of going on this trip. The maths teacher has had a problem with his passport and he has asked me to do him a favour and go on the recce (A recce is a preliminary trip just for one or maybe two staff members, without students. You spend your time working out how long it is to walk places, risk assess any activities, find out what train stops you get off at, take photos for the parents evening and so on). I don't particularly want to go, but as he's a mate, I will do him that favour. A geography teacher and I get on a flight to Frankfurt.

The maths teacher has booked the flights and we arrive in Frankfurt Hahn airport, which is basically an empty Toys 'r' Us. It's just a warehouse and we can see the guy take our baggage off the cart and put it on the carousel, which I can only guess has a team of hamsters manning the belt.

Problem one: Frankfurt Hahn is around a three-hour drive to the city centre of Frankfurt, and our hotel. Having thought we could just jump on an underground train, we are now going through the ball-ache of booking a coach in three hours' time. We find a pub. If you were planning on flying to London, you would be pretty annoyed if the flight that was booked for you landed in Cardiff.

We go to the hotel and take some photos, find our way to the train station, time the walk, find the coach park, and so forth. We find an Irish bar and stay in there for the next six hours. Frankfurt is not a nice place. We are accosted by several tramps and feel totally unsafe throughout our time there. We worry about our student's safety and definitely think they shouldn't be left outside with only remote supervision.

We go for a visit to the zoo; Frankfurt Zoo is awesome. Germany really know how to do a good zoo. In the bat exhibit, it is obviously pitch black, with bats flying everywhere. The enclosure is extremely dark; dark enough for me to hide in there before jumping out at my mate. I forget my mates' recent heart murmur and remember not to do it again.

On the last day before we fly home, we have a bit of time to ourselves and I suggest checking out the local football stadium. We go to Eintracht, Frankfurt's ground, on the tram and walk to the stadium. The stadium is slightly different to your average European stadium and the gate is about a mile to the actual ground, through a lot of woodland. If you haven't ever been there, it is stunning.

On our way to the ground there is a bit of a commotion up ahead and a lot of camera crews. The first team are training and my friend and I have the privilege of watching for three hours. We watch the press conference and also follow some cleaners into the stadium for a truly unique experience. It's one of the best days of my life and it wouldn't have ever happened unless I went on this stupid recce.

With about a week to go before the trip, I receive an e-mail with all the details, and the groups the staff will have. To my surprise my name is on as one of the group leaders. I tell the trip leader that there has been a mistake and in no way, shape or form, I am going back to Frankfurt and give up a week of my life to go there again. I'd reminded them that I had only done the recce as a favour in order for the trip leader to have all the information they need. Now that the trip leader has their passport all sorted, there is no need for me to be there.

He says, "And you tell me this now?!?" There has been a mix up but at no point have I said I would go on this trip.

Before I know it, I'm in the head's office again. She's telling me I have to go to Frankfurt. I've explained that I do not want to go (bear in mind this is during half-term) and she is a foot away from my face shouting "Do you think I'm going to pay for you to go on a jolly?!". I tell her I didn't want to go on the recce in the first place and I was doing it as a favour to the school. She changes her tone and says through gritted teeth, "We would really appreciate it if you would go to Frankfurt". She knows she can't make me go and her trying to be nice is actually causing her pain. I submit, and assure her I will go, as I weigh up what would happen if I didn't. This would likely be something along the lines of the head making my time here even more awkward and she would definitely find a way of getting me in more trouble.

We get on the coach to Frankfurt and I am incredibly unhappy. I tell the new trip leader that I had no interest of being on this trip, but for the good of the students, I will do my best.

Day one. We have our walking tour of the financial district and I am trying to be as enthusiastic as I can, which ends up being a little over the top. The tour guide says we are off to look at some buildings and I shout "YES! BUILDDDIIINNNGGSSS!" I feel a bit bad (and childish), but I'm trying to make this a little less dull. At one point, the guide says "The Deutsche Bank is the second largest bank in the whole of Germany". I pretend to faint a little and say "Oh mate.....

please tell me, what is the biggest?" He ignores me and I feel like the idiot I am.

Normally on trips, the group leader may buy you a little something, just to say 'thank you', which is always nice. Normally you have given up a week of your holidays. I'm hoping for something Eintract Frankfurt related, as I feel like a bit of a fan now. The trip leaders' friend gets a decent amount of makeup and a new make-up bag as that has been the majority of their conversations all week; my mate gets a set of books relating to the book he is currently reading. I am given a Nerf Gun, which I give to the first kid I see. Glad to see the school clearly understands my interests, and appreciated my sacrifice.

## 20. TTFN

I've arrived at work with a corking hangover today. I lock the door of the disabled toilet and close my eyes. I wake up two hours later.

* * * * *

The heads PA is leaving and everyone (especially me) is happy about it. Attendance to her party is mandatory. We have a band playing in the school hall; the speeches are un-heckled, which is a real shame.

The old head has arrived to say his goodbyes and thanks, and it is well known around the schooling world that he has been fired from his most recent job. He has basically taken a 'Good' school into 'Special Measures' in a pretty rapid turn of events.

He comes up to me and says, "I can't believe you are still here!" I reply, "Thanks for your vote of confidence... how are you anyways? Keeping yourself busy?"

I enjoyed that.

\*   \*   \*   \*   \*

It's snowing quite badly and it's time for my yearly haircut. I've gone to my local barbers and it's great in there; decent music is always playing, my loyalty card is almost full, the barbers are friendly, and it's relatively cheap. I love my barbers.

Whilst getting my haircut with my eyesight being the way it is, I can't really see what's going on around me and when he asks, "Is this all okay?" I normally just say yes, not to offend him. I'm very British. There is a loud knock at the window and the barber asks me "Do you know these lads?" When I put my glasses back on I can see that I sadly do know "these lads". All 12 of them. Laden with snowballs. Like I said earlier, kids would have no problem tripping you over and kicking the shit out of you in the snow. You can't do anything, as you can't seem weak in front of them or give them a good story to tell their mates.

I kindly ask the barber if he has a back door and run the mile home.

\*   \*   \*   \*   \*

We have a girl with us today who has hospitalised a teacher. As the teacher has gone to open her classroom door, the girl, messing around, has come charging through the door, breaking the teachers arm in four places.

She still thinks it's funny, but because this girls' parents are really difficult and ringing the school to complain a lot, the school are looking after her, which leaves the teacher incredibly angry.

The girl is given a one-day suspension.

\* \* \* \* \*

Parent's day again today. I have prepared really well this time. A big bottle of still liquids (no noise). Chewy snacks (again, no noise), laptop and extension lead with headphones. Biggest coat I could find (blanket) and I have set up in the PE cupboard for the day, where they store the high jump mats. I wake up around 5-o-clock; an hour later than I was supposed to leave.

\* \* \* \* \*

I've been called to a lesson as a student has got annoyed with another student and dragged him off his chair and started punching him. Its an IT lesson so this is a surprise as students are normally incredibly engaged by glowing screens. I ask the student what caused the violence?

"He was taking the piss out of my Mum's website".

I worry that it's an Only Fans so I ask him what the website is on.

"She runs anger management courses".

Only one thing gets repeated through my head. "Don't laugh, don't laugh, don't laugh".

\*　　\*　　\*　　\*　　\*

One of the SEN kids has taken a bit of a shine to us and is coming up to our office to show us his work all the time. We are all really happy to see him and let him know how well he is doing. We are really proud of him and we want him to stay at our school and do well. He does have the tendency to flare up at times and become extremely violent. He has trigger words that cause him to 'flip'; a few of the more distasteful students have worked this out and are using it for their own entertainment. It's awful and really angers the staff; the students involved are fully put on the rack for it.

He has flared up at us a few times, arriving to us very angry, and we are doing our best to calm him down.

He has arrived today with, quite literally, a bang. He has only got 98% on his maths test. When looking through his test I have just read on the final blank page, "If you give this test anything less than 100%, I will kill your family".

Staff are mortified, and I've taken a photo.

\* \* \* \* \*

My colleague has complained of a bad back. I will be doing all the running for the near future. I don't mind that; I hate being cooped up in that room being called a wanker for a living. I am impatient at the best of times; I get bored and I just want to mess around. Placing me with the naughty kids was not always the best idea, when I get distracted easily. The other problem with being in the same little room with these students is that by the end of the day, it absolutely stinks.

When I get in my car to go home I realise that it is actually me. Poor kids.

\* \* \* \* \*

My colleagues new chair has arrived today. This will hopefully help with her back problems. It has been delivered to our office in a massive cardboard box. My mischief cogs are turning and I feel there is a good practical joke in this somewhere. I unbox the chair incredibly carefully and put it in the middle of the room. There has to be something.

Love it. I convince my colleague to sit in the box and lightly tape it up.

Now. I have told my colleague that I'm off to get a student to help me move the box. I'm going to double up this joke and take ages to find a student. Upon my return (20 minutes), Miss is still in the box. She is great. Always up for a bit of a laugh too, but helpfully quite naïve. A student and I go to pick up the box and a sweaty Miss jumps out and shouts "RAAAAaaaaaa" at the student and I absolutely wet myself. Hopefully that will keep me going for the day.

Me being me, I have managed to pick the only student in the school to have a recent heart murmur. After a few days, I am in the head's office being told off for unprofessionalism, which in my opinion is fair enough. I think it was worth it though.

## 21. Norfolk off

Stanislavski! There is nothing I don't know about him. He is basically a drama practitioner from Russia who invented the act of staying in character at all times. We always set it as work in our room when we have a student removed from drama. Which is often.

I visit the drama room and the teacher is fully in character as a little old lady and when I stop the lesson she refuses to stop her craft and talks to me in character. I need to take one of the students and do a bag search and she is asking me a lot of questions in the style of the old lady to impress her students. She soon changes when I say that the student is almost definitely in possession of a hunting knife.

\*    \*    \*    \*    \*

Wow. We have just completed the geography field trip to Norfolk. It has been awful on the coast, trying to draw pictures in the rain. It's not a lot of fun and the kids are more than making up for it by acting feral. Try teaching them about groynes and you will understand.

Firstly, we have a few really drunk students and we have searched their room for any sign of alcohol. Nothing in the bin, nothing in any bags, nothing out of the window. I'm starting to think they've drank it all. Whilst moving the bedding around, the pillow makes a watery noise, and some absolute genius has filled his inflatable pillow with vodka. He's definitely going to be suspended, but in all honesty, he should be very proud of himself.

The next day, we spend the day in the high street in the rain, watching kids count litter and ask people where they are from (all from the town we are in. Who would come and visit a seaside town in the rain?). One gentleman isn't particularly happy that our school is wandering around his town and has screamed at me and two other teachers. "Why don't you and your fucking kids get out of the fucking way! You are so rude!". I take the lead in front of the Head of geography and say calmly, "So, it's not rude shouting FUCKING KIDS in my face?". He asks for the name of our school and I plan what I will say in the meeting which will inevitably come.

Still quite annoyed by the rude man, I was walking down the high street and was going to nip into the arcade to cheer myself up. On the way down I had to walk alongside a white transit van due to the street being so narrow and the traffic meant we were travelling at the same speed. The driver leans out of the window and says something to me; I couldn't really hear him, so I ignore it and smile at him.

Ten yards later he says something else and I again smile as I have no idea what he is saying, but his demeanour suggests I'm doing something wrong. Another ten yards passes, and he says something else. I stop and say "WHAT!?! What is it?? What do you want?". The guy looked stunned and said in his quaint Norfolk accent "I wuz just sayin' I should've come down 'ere earlier coz there wouldn't 'ave been so much traffic". I am a horrible dickhead.

## 22. Master of the House

The time has come. Im an alcoholic. It's the first time I've admitted to myself. It will be time before I tell others as I'm incredibly embarrassed by it.

When I walk home now it is a good hours walk. I start by going to the local cricket club, then up the hill to the next pub. A couple in here before the longer walk to my local football club. People come and go from here, normally popping in on their way home from work. It's nice to hear about how their day has gone and compare it to my own. I will drink in here until they ask me not to anymore. I like that I don't know what might happen. Being the person I am, I will always bump into people and have a laugh. This blots out my daily struggles that bring me down; the mistakes I make in work; sitting near a phone waiting for it to ring and see what trouble I am in now. I drink way too much.... daily. I lie to myself too and say "its to help me sleep" but it isn't (even though it does). The last walk back to the pub I live in is almost over and I need to make a change. I need to do something about this but I am far too weak. I hate myself, I hate my job. What to do? Who to talk to?

The answers are nothing and no one.

\*     \*     \*     \*     \*

Since dating the music teacher she has really opened my eyes to a lot of things and now a new love of my life is musical theatre. I will not tell my mates about this as I think they will call me names.

The school has decided to do a production of Les Miserables. The best one!

I say I will help as I love the musical and I can spend more time with my girlfriend. I am not particularly trusted to do anything major and am tasked to painting bricks on the plywood barricade.

After the light success of Honk they have asked me to choreograph the musical number "Master of the House. To those of you who don't know, its a scene inside a pub. My absolute forte.

This goes well and involves Thenadier accidentally drinking a bottle of his own piss, and has a bit of audience participation.

It's gone so well in fact, they would like me to help out more. I've been given a line.

"You at the barricades listen to this! No one is coming to help you to fiiiiiighhht! You're own your own you have no chance, lay down your guns or die!".

Oh what's that? I have to sing it from the wings? My nerves are going but I hold my own... (ish). To this day this production is the best thing I've been involved in at work. It gets a lot of plaudits and everyone who comes are impressed with the production and the kids are unreal.

I've decided to step out of my comfort zone more.

*   *   *   *   *

My friend who is now quite important in the school as an assistant head, has asked for my help to run the school alumni.

This will involve running the Facebook group and trying to get guest speakers in to inspire the kids. We do have some really famous alumni; footballers, singers, DJ's, titans of industry, rugby players, golfers... it really is a good barrel to pick from.

The singer is the big one! She has appeared on TV a lot recently and was asked about her school days, and she talks about her bullying issues. It makes the school look bad but I feel quite sorry for her.

I contact her agent. I get no reply for a few weeks and try again. This goes on for a year. Finally, I hear back from the agent and we have more back and forth about her returning to school to do a bit of a speech. We manage to get a date where she is going to come in. This has been a year in the making and a lot of admin on my behalf. The date is set and I've organised rooming and also which kids will be lucky enough to get to listen to her.

The day comes and I am nervous. I do an announcement in our staff briefing to announce the arrival of her this afternoon and itinerary of the day. It's mainly the musical students and ones who will be going on to uni to do performing arts. I also throw in a kid who was misbehaving and bribed him.

I see her coming up the path with her agent and I rush down to reception to greet her. There is a buzz about the place and I'm incredibly proud that I've managed to sort all this.

I introduce myself and sort her out a name badge (this genuinely is a procedure to national treasures as well as people doing some plumbing work). I sign her in and go to the heads office as our first port of call.

Photographs are taken and some fairly cringe chit chat. I hurry them along a little as we need to get to the lecture theatre as we have 100 kids chomping at the bit. The head asks her if she could record herself saying what a great school it is and that you should want to come here. Her face drops and she has to awkwardly say no. This makes me incredibly annoyed as our star seems to be unhappy about the ambush and she seems a lot more closed off in her body language. At this point it makes me mad; it seems to be more about what we can get from you to make us look good and not what you can do to inspire our kids. I'm embarrassed.

I get her to the lecture theatre which is a fair walk, which gets a lot of attention from kids out of the windows of their maths classes. She's quite a stunner and I'm feeling a little smug.

We arrive and my friend is waiting, settling the students. "Thanks" he says to me, "Can you go and get us two cups of water?".

All this planning and work, it has taken nine words to make me feel useless again. Off I pop to get two cups of water, missing all the introduction and most of the first half. The second half goes really well and she genuinely is a delight.

After a while I escort her back to the reception and on the way she tells me how nervous she was. I say to her "I saw you at the V festival which had about 50,000 people". She replies "I know what I'm doing there. People have come to see me. I have no idea how 50 kids will act". I respond "Oh, you get used to it. The trick is to remember that you pretty much hate 90% of them".

I contemplate my joke where I plan to walk through the maths lesson with an entrance and an exit saying "for goodness sake, leave me alone, I'm not interested" whilst she follows behind saying "please, just call me!". I bottle it but say to my mates down the pub that I did this.

On reflection, I shouldn't have been so nervous. It turns out that she is one of the nicest people you will ever meet. She is a total inspiration to our students, and myself. She leaves and gives me a kiss on the cheek. She's great and so is life.

## 23. Can you hold on until 3:20?

I get a strange text from a mate to call him urgently. I find five minutes and give him a call. "You need to come to the hospital urgently, Dean is about to die and we are going to say goodbye". This news hits me like a tonne of bricks. We were only out the other day. It seems that he has septicaemia and the hospital are counting down the minutes. I speak to my boss and rush down to the absence officer and explain the situation.

"Can you wait until 3:20?"

It seems that I don't have a choice... I leave at 3:20. I say my goodbyes and talk to him a little, reassuring him that he can pull through. I'm balling my eyes out. We go to the pub and talk about old times and funny stories. Then wait for the text.

It never comes! Thank God.

* * * * *

My mate has started working here. Awesome stuff. I say mate... technically he's a guy that I know, I like, and he is here as as student support assistant. I used to play cricket and he was in a team in a lower league to mine. He's a nice guy and I'm glad he's here. I hope he's as good as what I think he is, as he has just come from working in a bank, he's a little bit older than me, but I know this is a good addition. I happen to know that his best mates' wife is the manager of the department he has joined. I'm glad it's not just me who has gotten a job through these means.

* * * * *

It's the beginning of the new school year and we have the obligatory safeguarding training and staff introductions. It's great to see the new staff and judge them on their suitability without even talking to them.

This is an all day thing. We sit in the school hall listening to the same training as last year. Radicalisation is a new one. In our leafy suburb I can't see there will be much call for it, but I'm happy to learn any new skills. I sit next to the history teacher that loves football. Today we will be picking our best ever football sides which have played in the Serie A and then footballers who could also be TV programmes. Sharp, Taggert, Dan Petrescu. We silently do this on a piece of paper at the back.

I hear my department get mentioned so I forget the comparison of Paolo Maldini to Franco Baresi and listen for a minute. To my surprise we have a new speaker on stage. An expert in his field and former drama specialist . He is trying to be funny whilst telling us all that we are doing our jobs wrong. At one point he got a volunteer to put toothpaste back in a tube which was something to do with teaching. He tells this long winded story about him reading to kids in a behaviour department. Fair play, he is explaining that these kids have never been read to before.

After a while I'm back at my desk doing some admin to the job that I am actually paid to do.

In walks the head with our expert.

"Do you ever read to kids in here?" he says, using his hands a bit too much.

"No, of course not". I reply receiving a stabbing to the eye from my headteacher's evil look

"Why not?" he asks.

"Well, we've been told to be silent all day and only interact with the kids on matters relating to their classwork. If we read them stories they might want to come back!".

They both leave after a short tour.

RING RING... "Can you pop down to see the head".

## Chapter 24. Shite, Shite, Baby!

The SLT member in charge of timetabling who continually gets it wrong, yet keeps his job, is doing the briefing today about RAP sheets (I still to this day do not know what this means).

He has decided in his infinite wisdom to do a rap to emphasise his point.

I do not say this lightly. It is the worst thing I've ever seen.

\* \* \* \* \*

I decide to go "Sober for October" its going to be hard but I want to prove I can do it. After a few days I get a £10 donation from the kid who I mentor. He's clearly googled me and then donated some of his pocket money. I ring home and ask his Mum if this was ok. She says that he talks about me a lot. She thanks me a lot for all I've done for him. I tell her I will continue to do so until he leaves at the end of year 11 or even sixth form.

\* \* \* \* \*

It's been a while since something has gone wrong. Ive kept my head down and I've been working really hard. The head of house job has come up again.

In for a penny. I feel it can't possibly go as badly as last time.

The same process happens. Two interviews with students and the head, and a written task. The main point of the interview is how you would inspire staff who don't want to get involved, and what you do when they don't. It's pretty straightforward and I make a good effort; lo and behold, I am now a middle leader.

I have literally no idea how this has happened. I am going to make my house the best it can be. I'm full of hope for this. Finally something has gone well.

Undoubtedly I'll fuck it up, but I'm going to enjoy the responsibility (and extra dosh) for as long as I can.

*****

My first house assembly is coming soon; prep has already started and I'm already getting nervous.

At this point in this book and my life ,everything is going extremely well. My girlfriend and I are flying; she is genuinely the best thing that has ever happened to me. My friends say I fall in love too easily and I know what they are saying, but this could be it. This could be the one. She inspires me to do better not only as a man but as a staff member. My job is looking a lot better and I'm comfortable in terms of life and money.

What could possibly go wrong?

## 25. Start spreading the news.

Working within a school you can easily get pigeon-holed . If you are doing well at one job, you are passed over for promotion, as they would like you to continue to be good at the job you're in. This happens a lot. It's sad and I've seen really good people leave as they are continually looked over as they would prefer to hire someone not as good externally, so the staff numbers are still the same.

It's crap! Really really crap.

\*     \*     \*     \*     \*

My first house assembly has arrived and I have planned it to the nth degree, even my ad libbed parts are scripted. I talk about teamwork and give out competition results, and tell them all about upcoming events. It goes superbly to plan and we even play a mass participation game which gets them all up and happy, all to the tune of Gangnam Style. God, I'm proud of myself. The headteacher watches on throughout with her arms folded. But the phone never rings.

Do you know what? I might have nailed this job. Let's just keep my head down and see where it goes.

\*   \*   \*   \*   \*

It's the big one. The trip to end all trips. My girlfriend has been asked to take over the leadership of the year 11 trip to New York, twice a year, during the half-terms. Only the best students are allowed to go and its always over-subscribed.

She has asked me to come. I'm elated. I'm sure this is because of my new work ethic but may also be to save money on rooms.

Taking 50 kids to a bus stop can be eventful, but taking 50 to one of the most protected countries in the world, in one of the busiest cities in the world, is an absolute pleasurable nightmare.

At Heathrow, before the wheels have left the tarmac, I quickly realise students in our school are given way too much money by their parents. They are already throwing on Armani belts, Louis Vuitton luggage and Nike Air luggage tags, bought at the airport itself. Thankfully our students are fairly well behaved, so the flight itself goes off without a hitch. Their downfall however, is their lack of responsibility when Mummy and Daddy aren't around to tie their shoelaces.

Every child needs to keep hold of their passport as they need to get through security with it; we can't hold on to them like we would a theatre ticket. In spite of the staff walking around the seats of our students three times before we have to put our seatbelts on to land, and reminding them to pack up everything they need, there's still a child that leaves their passport on the plane. By the time we get to security, they only just realise. The plane is being cleaned and ready for boarding the next set of passengers back to London, and we have to hold 50 very excitable students in a luggage area while we wait for the poor air stewards to hunt down this passport. When it's finally found, the child is reasonably humble and embarrassed. Safe to say they were perfectly behaved for the entire trip... although they did lose their metro card on the second day.

It must be -20 degrees here. The wind whistles down the avenues and hits you in the face like a cricket bat made of slush puppy. Of course, like any good trip leaders, we made sure to share a packing list with our students, and advised them of the wintry weather, so that they (and their parents) would pack the right thermal gear and jackets. When we get to the hotel lobby we all realise that none of this briefing has penetrated the minds of our students. It is genuinely -21 now with the windchill. If you went out with wet hair you would be able to snap it off. Students have opted for converse trainers, leggings, crop top with exposed midriff with a denim jacket. I say to the leader of this girl gang that they could actually die if they go out like this. They go back upstairs to get jumpers.

The PE teacher has decided not to pack a hat as he doesn't look good in them.

My outfit consists of wooly hat, scarf, under armour bottom layer, long sleeve t-shirt, jumper, coat with hood, socks, football socks, jeans and walking boots. I look like a Michelin man, which isn't great as I'm pretty fat already. I consider walking down Fifth Avenue stepping on cars and attacking the Ghostbusters.

On the first evening, we walk the students in the bitter cold to Times Square, and spot the people carrying snakes and grown men dressed like superheroes bugging you for photos and money. We give our students the best guidance we can about timings, what to avoid, and how to keep safe. We point out the good shops, and off we go to get our first meal and break from the kids in 24 hours at the nearest Irish bar as tradition (so I'm told).

When we meet back at Times Square a few hours later, the girls have removed their jumpers and are back to bare midriffs. One is crying because she is so cold; it's hard not to say I told you so. Next day is a different story. They are all dressed like Arctic explorers and the PE teacher has got himself a new Yankees bobble hat... he looks fine.

Our hotel has a fantastic location - right opposite Madison Square Gardens, and adjacent to Macy's. It's great for the early morning breakfast, and a quick stroll before it all gets really busy. The downfall is unfortunately the hotel itself. I was thankful that the room allocated to a member of staff was the one with the mouse in; she was initially from the countryside up North so she took the challenge on with gusto. The trickier situation was the volume of dogs. The US-style Crufts was happening in the same week as our trip, in Madison Square Gardens, and it appears that our hotel is the exclusive dog hotel for the entire of New York. We have fluffy ones, angry ones, tiny ones in cages... you name them. The kids don't mind so much. The owners of the dogs are probably more mortified than anyone, when our kids go running up and start stroking them and fluffing all their fur the wrong way. The PE teacher has quite a phobia of dogs. Safe to say we don't see him in the hotel lobbies so much. He meets us outside.

Day two and students are up at 7am ready for museum day. First on the checklist is the 9/11 museum (this is so humbling; a must for anyone going to NYC). The students have been great and we send them off outside to the waterfalls that have every name of the people who died as part of the 9/11 terrorist attacks. We send them on some activities to spot if anyone shares their surname, and to find the person from our hometown who was tragically involved. We leave flowers and take photos and my heart soars when I see the greatness in our kids.

Next up is the Museum of Natural History. This is a gigantic museum, with lots of fake things that existed at one time, but doesn't anymore. It's far too big to tackle. The best bit is the planetarium. As soon as you get comfy, it goes dark, and a soothing voice tells you about all the stars you can see above you. Naturally after all the travel and looking after these children day and night, I fell asleep. My girlfriend nudges me as I'm snoring; I apologise and fall back to sleep immediately and I am nudged awake again. I apologise again. My partner tells me it wasn't her and I turn to see quite an annoyed Jamaican lady.

Day three is a visit to MOMA: one of the greatest collections of art in the world. We walk past the kids in the lobby frantically trying to get on the WiFi. We return two hours later and all but three students have seen one painting.

We walk back through Central Park towards the Dakota building, through the memorial garden for John Lennon: Strawberry Fields. This is my chance to shine and I give the students a big talk about the murder of John Lennon and what he meant to the world. One student asks if I used to run after The Beatles; I'm sure he knows I was born in the 80's. I feel I've done enough during my impassioned speech about Mr Lennon to get invited back on the next trip, and I'm sure the five tourists that stopped and listened got a lot out of it too. There's a busker playing Beatles songs, and the students sing and dance to him; there's that heart soaring moment again. How do these kids do it?!

It's finally here. The day they have been waiting for. Day four: shopping day. We've held them back all week, making sure they were bringing as limited money as possible out, so they could feed themselves all week, and now the day of reckoning is finally here. It's a muggers dream; if only they knew.

The students know they can shop up and down Fifth Avenue, and they have already Googled exactly where each shop is, and planned out their route with their mates. By the time we meet up with them later, they have bought New York. We add up their potential purchases and guess they have spent roughly £25,000 between them. I'm sickened in all honesty. One child has bought himself and his brother a present. I asked to see it, thinking it may be a nice

Obama bobblehead. He opened his bag to show me two iPads.

Day five is the final day. Students are worn out. Teachers were worn out days ago. But it's skyscraper day; the day in which we all get to look in awe at the beauty and interest in NYC. We go to the top of the Rockerfeller, the Empire State Building, the newly built Freedom Tower, and a boat trip around the Statue of Liberty for good measure. We finish off with the students desperately trying to fit all their purchases into their suitcases, and weighing them all to make sure they can get them on the plane. We are so relieved when we hand them back to the parents, and head back home. Just as our heads hit the pillow, a phone call on the emergency mobile; a child has left their brand new Timbaland boots on the bus from Heathrow.

## 26. SEIZE THE DAY!

One of the loveliest cover teachers is leaving to become a life coach. We all wish her well. She says something really nice about me in her leaving speech which has made me think even more of her.

She tells us all that she was undecided on whether she was going to leave or not, but said "Carpe Diem". The head immediately jumps in and shouts "SEIZE THE DAY". Everyone is silent, and confused. To me, it's hilarious. How pathetic must you be, to prove that you understand the fundamentals of Latin.

(I write this four years later and I still shout "SEIZE THE DAY" anytime I hear Carpe Diem said or written down. At least she didn't start fucking rapping.)

\* \* \* \* \*

It's coming up to the end of the sixth form term and we are all looking forward to the pranks they play. It's normally quite an honour to have your car wrapped in cellophane. It means you've meant something to them. This year is brilliant. On my way in to school I enter the sixth form common room to see what they've done. Last year they left thousands of cups of water on the floor and in the middle was an inflatable boat. it must have taken an awful lot of planning, but this year may have got out of hand.

They have absolutely trashed the place. Possibly causing criminal damage. Tables are snapped, a window is cracked, rubbish has been tipped over the floor and a lot of loo roll and silly string has been emptied everywhere. My personal favourite was a pot of couscous tipped out like a sandcastle on the Head of sixth's computer. All sixth form celebration activities have been cancelled and the photos have made it to the local paper through social media. It's a bit much, but the head saying she is going to involve the police is way too much. Surely we are here to teach students right from wrong. They got it wrong on this occasion, and that's on us.

* * * * *

My mate who was recently employed as an SSA, has now become an assistant to all the heads of year. I'm pleased he's doing well for himself, but after a while it is being proved that he is either out of his depth or incredibly lazy. Rather than having my 'Netflix and Snacks' day on parents day, I choose to help him out instead and get him caught up on all his work. I pull him out of the depths of his backlog. We plan a round of golf together and in a fitness push, start using the school gym in the evenings. This could be really great for both of us.

## 27. This is your eleventh warning.

I have been asked to run a trip. This is an honour - and a massive burden. I am taking 109 year 7 students to Bideford on an adventure activity trip, and I get the honour of being trip leader. Its a lot of responsibility and I can't believe I've been trusted with it.

Luckily my girlfriend helps me with a lot of the admin and makes me a big to do list. She's very good at that. Luckily most stuff has been done before and I can just copy and paste a lot of the risk assessments from a previous year and change all the dates. I also do the school assemblies and start assembling a team of staff to come with me.

One thing I've never had to deal with before are the finance team.

I get a call to go to the finance office. I get there to three stern looking faces as I have got the budget slightly wrong. The main one tells me "this is your first warning, the budget is wrong".

"Oh! I'm so sorry. What is it that I got wrong?". The finance officer tells me about tax or something and I've slightly undercharged all the students. Luckily the letters haven't gone out so they are easily amended. I also realise later through my copy and pasting, that this was never brought up to the previous trip leaders. Just me. Strange.

I ask out of interest (and perhaps a little cheekily), "What happens on my second warning or third warning?"

"Well, nothing. It's just not good enough."

My dickhead side kicks in. "I don't like the way you're talking to me, so this is your seventh warning".

"Do you want me to cancel this trip?", she retorts. This has really got me going now.

"By all means! I don't get paid for this! Perhaps let's work together and help me out, rather than give me warnings.".

This is the last time we ever spoke.

The trip is going really well; in spite of my worries of my leadership skills, I'm starting to settle into the role. One evening, I ask one of the group leaders if I could borrow her for a minute, and I walk off outside. She follows me, looking a bit sheepish. "Oh my god what have I done?", she says, appearing panicked and white-faced. "Oh! Nothing! You're awesome. I just needed a cigarette. Can I nab one from you please?"

In this moment I realised that no matter who you are or what you do, you will always be worried about the people above you. I apologise to her a lot and then I'm overly nice to her for the rest of the trip. I'm glad I'm not alone with my anxieties.

The trip goes swimmingly and I even get a gift from a parent, which is a first. As support staff, you don't get many gifts from parents, so its always a nice surprise when you do. I'm fed up of my girlfriend bringing home flowers and candles every half-term. It's so rare to get a power cut; what is the point?

\* \* \* \* \*

The highly autistic student has been sent to us today as he is refusing to do another test. I sit with him for three hours before eventually letting him go home with 0% on his test, but also with an incredibly good drawing of me with knives through my eyes. Everyone's a critic.

My second house assembly is coming up on "triumph against adversity". You can pretty much say anything you like in an assembly as long as you mention the title a few times. I've decided to borrow the smoke machine from the drama department to add a little atmospheric tension to the next mass game.

I am told I'm not allowed due to one student in 300 having asthma. I decide in future to ask for forgiveness rather than permission.

## 28. We're soaring, we're flying.

Life is going pretty well. The music teacher and I have moved in together. She's great, but working and living with someone can have its draw backs. In bed the other night she asked me if I'd seen the year 9's attendance data. I hadn't.

My drinking has been curbed as I address living in the real world. I'm enjoying seeing things and having experiences that I've never had before. Did you know there is a time before 7 am? Unbelievable.

\*    \*    \*    \*    \*

I'm doing better at work too (funny how these things seem to come together) and I've taken to mentoring some students. I feel really involved in improving their lives. I've also set up a mentoring system where sixth formers are helping year 7's with homework and some light reading. It's going great. I feel like I'm actually making a difference to children's lives. This is what I'm here for.

I have recently set up a lot of sharable online paperwork where we can identify patterns in poor behaviour. It's 80% boys in Key Stage 3 after break time, which is slightly odd. It must be something in the bread and cheese combinations offered in the canteen. The deputy head is incredibly impressed with my analysis, and it is shared amongst the school. I go a step further and look at our on-call data (an on-call is when a teacher contacts you and asks you to remove a student). This helps teachers who are getting a lot of on-calls, so we can provide them with support in the classroom. It also makes their head of department aware that they could probably do with popping in to a few lessons and keeping the naughty kids at bay.

Jumping from one lily-pad to another, I'm off on another idea. Every lesson of every day, I have the data to show where students are getting kicked out of lessons, and by what teachers. If I can get to them before that lesson and speak to them, chances are that the positive conversation before the lesson will mean they won't be removed.

Inspired by 'Strike it Lucky' I call it the Hotspot System. It is used school wide even to this day (don't fact-check that). Im absolutely flying right now and this shows just what I can actually do when I put my mind to positive things.

*   *   *   *   *

More good news! My lazy mate has been promoted to head of a rival house! I can really only see the house system getting better and a few of the more experienced leaders have started following my lead of making the house assemblies the highlight of the term. The deputy head was seen laughing his way through my last assembly. He has also suggested selling tickets.

I've noticed I haven't told a story about a stupid thing a student has done for a while so my PE teacher tells me about an incident with a student who was regularly in my room. The child was caught masturbating in the swimming pool showers. "Fucking hell mate", I say. "How good was the lesson?".

\* \* \* \* \* \*

We have a student currently in school that's known as a flight risk or a 'runner'. That is, any sign of trouble, he will just run. He doesn't have the bottle to run home or to the shops. He will be on school site somewhere, so some poor guy has to go and hunt him down. That would be me. Having been a student at this school myself, and not the greatest with my behaviour, I know a lot of the hiding places already. He never goes for a toilet or a cupboard. He finds empty classrooms or somewhere sneakier, like pushing four wheelie bins in a square and sitting in the middle (I was quite impressed with that one). We get the call on the phone, or we get buzzed on our beepers (that's right, beepers) and we call the office to check in as to where to go, or we answer the call ourselves and respond accordingly. Now that our 'runner' knows the process, he has turned this into a game, and enjoys the chase. The problem is, you look a bit of a prick at school, running around as a staff member, unless you are in a PE kit. And when you catch up to the student, what can you do? It's like when you watch a dog chase a squirrel. If they ever catch hold of them, they sort of stand still, not really sure what to do, so let them go again, hungry for the chase. What am I going to do with a student? I cannot throw him to the floor, cuff him and march him back to my office.

You just have to hope they make the right decisions. They never do.

The other day he went running from maths. He didn't see me from my office, but I spotted him hiding in the big hedge outside one of the blocks for a minute, before deciding against it, and off he went.

He lead me a merry dance, running all around the school, only to be waiting in my office when I returned spinning on my office chair and pretending to stroke a cat saying, "Sir, I've been expecting you." It was too funny to remain angry at this one. Little shit.

'The Runner' has maths. He will most definitely be running from this one. I pre-empt the hedge-hiding. I get a buzz from my beeper and I call the office and I'm there quick as a flash… hiding in his hedge.

I know it's a little sad to be trying your hardest to outwit children, but I need this student to know that we are one step ahead of him, if we are going to get through to him at all. Also, it's going to be hilarious to see how scared he is going to be when I jump out of his hedge.

It's only gone and paid off! He has absolutely shit himself. Shame he has run away again now. That went against all of my plans. But of course you would run away when you're scared, wouldn't you. I hadn't quite thought of that. If only I had a SWAT team to surround him as part of my plans. Shame he ran away. I probably needed to tell him about the consequences of his actions.

**29. Part of the job.**

A really horrible thing has happened today, and I'm struggling with it. A student's Mum has sadly died in an accident, and I've been sent to collect him and take him to the deputy heads office, where the deputy head and his Dad are waiting. It's a long walk to his classroom and so much is going through my head. His life is going to be so difficult from now on, and I can't help but want to hug him. I obviously can't do that, and I don't want to be the one who breaks the awful news. As I enter his classroom and say his name to collect him and tell him to get his stuff, there is confusion all around and a lot of kids are asking "What for?". I ask him to follow me as we have to see the deputy head. The teacher is aware of the situation, and ushers us out quickly to try and keep the muttering down.

He follows me, asking me what's it about as he's obviously worried he might have done something wrong. I play dumb and tell him

I'm not sure, but not to worry about it too much as he's not in trouble.

I arrive at the office and show the student inside, who is incredibly confused and worried when he sees his Dad there. I put my hand on his shoulder and quietly leave. I would hate to imagine what happened in that room from there.

### 30. "So Ted, I hear you're a racist."

"FIGHT! FIGHT! FIGHT! FIGHT!" The worst thing you can hear on duty. And this, my friends, is a good one. The crowd is getting larger, and more phones are coming out of kids pockets ready to film it and chuck it on social media for all to see. Personally, I feel that the kids holding the phones should be in just as much trouble as the kids actually fighting; no doubt they have been coerced in to fighting, and then the students with phones have the opportunity to make the school look bad if they forward this video around the world.

I'm first on the scene, and it's fine. I have split the two brawlers up; they both look relieved that I have, and it's now time to disperse the crowd. I send one of the perpetrators to the behaviour room and advise him sit in my office. He shouts at me, "What about him?!" I said "I will deal with him next. I just need you to go so I can start confiscating phones and getting rid of the crowd." He leaves and gets about 20 yards before coming back and screams at me "You're only sending me up there first because I'm black!". Inner groan. It's definitely not for this reason, but I have literally no way of proving this to him, or the crowd that are beginning to pick up their phones again.

I walk with him to the behaviour room, ignoring his cries of racism. I don't want to explain myself in any way as through fear of getting it wrong. His friends are in tow now shouting "RACIST!" at me. I ask them to go away and imagine the headlines as I keep my head high and refuse to defend myself. I take the child straight to the deputy headteacher, explain the situation, and the accusations of racism. I leave the student with him and begin to gather written statements from some of the crowd who I know are good kids, who will likely tell the truth and are quite happy to grass people up. I write a full four-page report on this, and cover all bases to prove that I wasn't being racist.

I then get a call from another school to say that the video has reached them already, and send the video to us via e-mail.

Upon watching the video I have decided to lose some weight.

\* \* \* \* \* \*

It's sports day and for once, it isn't raining. Nothing worse than a cancelled sports day; lots of annoyed kids in PE kit, running absolutely wild, and disappointed teachers having to teach their lessons instead of basking in the glorious sunshine. In our infinite wisdom, we have decided to have a house vs. house relay race. I have obviously taken the 4th leg, as I like the attention (even if I'm losing I could do the worm or something).

The gun blasts and we're off: all four houses are giving it their all. My house are a long way in the lead, but I am up against the super fit English teacher who fancies himself as a bit of a... it's easier to say he fancies himself.

Our house wins, and the four runners are celebrating, jumping around, chanting our house name for all to hear. We are mobbed by approximately 400 students ; it is pure joy and an amazing feeling.

The English teacher shakes my hand and says "If there were ten more meters I would have beaten you". I'm happy that a few kids hear my reply, "Yeah, and if there were ten meters less I would have beaten you by more". One student tells me it was a sick burn! I think that was a good thing.

Later on in the week, the lovely lady in charge of reprographics has blown up a big photo of me crossing the line with the other team in my wake, and put it up in the staff room. Mr Speedy has been written across it. I am referred to as this for almost a week. I'm walking a bit taller at the moment.

## 31. And Heskey makes it five.

More trips coming up. It seriously is the best part of my job; seeing the world for free. It also means I don't have to buy my own food for a few days. Money is tight when you're as thirsty as I am.

We're off to Munich on another maths trip. I have been promised a trip to the Olympic Stadium along with one to the Allianz. I am uber-excited. We have a good group of kids; no little idiots. Just the good ones, and all are very appreciative. At the end of the day, who puts their name forward for a maths trip unless you're a good kid.

We wander around doing maths-related things. We've been to the stock exchange and the BMW museum, but upcoming is the Olympic Stadium. We enter the stadium, which is steeped in history, and I can't help but tell our tour guide what I was doing when Germany lost 5-1 to England in this very place. I miss out the details where I drank a pint of Stella topped up with red wine and fell off a table. After the changing rooms, we are asked to line up and we as staff stand at the back. I've done quite a lot of stadium tours. You usually experience the feeling of walking out to a big game, and then you sit on the subs benches and imagine what it's like. This time is different. This time our tour guide.... has a ball!

We are lead out on to the pitch, and to the centre circle. I'm already gobsmacked we are even allowed onto the pitch, and I'm walking on in disbelief. We line up like we are about to hear the anthems. We are then told we can have a kick around for 30 minutes or so. Everyone gets involved, and a large German crowd have started to watch us from the terraces, cheering if a goal is scored. I fancy a bit of this. I turn to the head of maths and then full "Brian Glover" in Kes, I'm heading in to the box as the ball has gone out wide. The cross is delivered perfectly on to my unusually large head, and nestles in the stanchion (me being at least 15 stone and a foot taller than my defensive rival did help slightly). I hear a big cheer from the crowd and I'm off, cupping my ears to the crowd as I head towards the corner. At this point I remember where I am and what happened here, and I stop to do the Emile Heskey celebration, where I pretend to putt an invisible golf ball towards the corner flag. I've learnt another lesson today. "Wichser" is German for wanker. You live and learn.

The trip goes pretty well and I am continually more and more proud of my header. In the evening, the SLT leader has confiscated two pizzas from a kids room; it turns out that they disliked the food in the German hostel so much that they had made the decision to work out how to order and pay for a pizza or two, so they don't go hungry. I also think they did it to look cool as well. Personally I'm pretty proud of them! Unfortunately the SLT leader announces she is annoyed that the students did this, and asks what I would have done. I reply that I would let them have the pizzas. She starts scowling and stating it's a safeguarding issue, as we don't know who the person is delivering the pizza to their rooms. I shake my head and decide not to say anything, but also let my room mate know over night that paedophile pizza delivery people would probably be bad for any Italian restaurant business.

One slight hiccup. We have been waiting a little while for our plane to be ready to board... we've been sat on the floor of the airport for a good few hours. However, we can see the pilot and the air staff have just boarded, and we know we are next. Suddenly, some of our students run up to us and tell us that a child has a nose bleed. We don't think too much of this... my girlfriend (yes, she's on the trip too), pops down to the toilets to check in on him, and keep one ear out for the tannoy asking us to board.

However, it just doesn't seem to stop. It's like a slow-running tap. The tannoy announcement has just come to say we can board, but there's no way he can board like this. I myself at this point have been tricked by a German barman in to having a steiner of strong German lager with the question "Would you like a ladies-size beer or a German beer?".

This feeling of being half cut has quickly left me now and I am in full professional mode as we are now dealing with an odd situation where we've had to make the decision that he can't fly home tonight, and needs to go to the hospital. The bleed hasn't stopped for over half an hour, and we are running out of options. I look around our staff group: 1: SLT female, can't do it, 2: maths teacher with three kids at home, can't do it, 3: my girlfriend, or 4: me: male and kidless. Shit!

I get in the ambulance and ask my girlfriend to sort my baggage out the other side. We drive down the autobahn at 120mph. We have several hours in hospital and I am liaising with the parents, school, airport and my very helpful girlfriend who is trying to organising flights and accommodation, whilst dropping off all the other students with their families back at school. I decide against the accommodation, as I can't share a room with the lad. I could be mistaken for a pizza delivery boy. After his treatment (his nose was quarterized and given splints and cotton to stop the bleed) I decide we just find somewhere in the airport to sleep, so we can get on the quickest plane home. However, at this point, I've realised I'm the only person responsible for this child, and I'm petrified he will either get kidnapped or start bleeding again whilst I snore away. I sit for 5 hours while he sleeps on a load of benches I've moved together in a dark and empty gate; imagine Tom Hanks in The Terminal; you get the idea. The desk finally opens and British Airways got us on the first flight back to Blighty. A very happy

Mum and Dad were at the airport to greet us and take us home. I sleep for two days.

\

## 32. The modern child is sometimes troubled.

I do not say this lightly, when I say that this was the worst situation I had to deal with whilst working at a school. I have received a call from reception to say that a member of the public has spotted four of our students in the woods... drunk. She's added that she thinks one of them is in a seriously bad way. It is currently 9am. My mind and body all click in, and I am now in charge of this situation. I'm going to need female and male members of staff, a mini bus with driver, a mobile phone and access to parents phone numbers.

This is not great.

I've got my female member of staff, who happens to be a safeguarding lead. I've located the keys for the minibus, found someone who can drive it, and within five minutes of the call, I've worked out the best place to travel and park to get to their location. We arrive to find four year 8 girls.

Year 8 is 12 to 13 years old. They have stolen whatever booze they can from their parents cabinets, and have decided to skip school and get drunk; this has got out of hand quickly. One of them is borderline unconscious and has thrown up a lot. We get the kids into the mini bus and happen across one of the parents whilst walking his dog. He is mortified and embarrassed, and he's started to cry.

Thankfully, he lives close by, and we get her home. He takes care of her and I've asked him to update us on her welfare. Three left to sort out. We don't want to take them onto school site and have drunk girls in our corridors. We want them either at home or in hospital, if they are too far cut. We park up with all girls safely in the back and I call the parents to get them collected.

"Hello is that Mrs Smith…"

"Yes, who is this?"

"I'm calling from your daughters school."

"Oh! Is everything ok?"

"There is no easy way to say this, but your daughter seems like she has had quite a bit of alcohol this morning. Could you possibly come to the cricket club car park to collect your daughter."

"I'm on my way".

In this time, we have found out the reason behind the scenario we find ourselves in today. One of the girls has coerced the other three in to an experimentation and self-harm party. It sounds pretty dark. I question why these girls would think that this is a good activity, and even more so, that I live in a world where this activity could even be conjured up. It's just incredibly sad. There are no winners here. We are all leaving worse off.

Mum No.1 turns up and shouts at the other two girls for leading her daughter astray, which judging by the fallout, is fair enough.

Mum No.2 is deciding to deal with matters at home and apologises profusely to us.

Mum No.3 crosses her arms and says to her daughter, "Wait till I get you home". The student looks at her and says calmly, "Oh fuck off you cunt". I would hate to be either of these two later. We return back to school and do the designated paperwork. For a moment while I get some time to myself, I allow myself a few tears after the adrenaline rush, and the sadness of the situation. I was glad of the effort I put in, and so relieved that the member of public rang in. I felt positive that I had done the right thing; I followed procedure well and thought on my feet, and all these girls (apart from probably girl and Mum No.3) were now safe.

Later on in the day, my phone rings. It's the Dad of the girl I dropped off first. He's now had time to think, and he's furious... with me! He's angry because it wasn't reported that his daughter wasn't at school. This is basically just a timing issue; the registers and phone calls are all done for students that are absent without a reason. She was on the list but the call isn't made until after 9.30am (and correctly so). I am getting a shedload of abuse from this bloke, and I'm remaining as professional as possible, but I'm also incredibly annoyed and sad about the situation. I ask him to politely ring the main reception and ask for a meeting with the head. My work here is done.

### 33. You can't see me!

I've decided to play to my strengths. In my next assembly, I will be wrestling a student. I have brought in an initiative that the highest performing tutor group get to choose my walk-on music, and they happen to have chosen John Cena's entrance music. I absolutely love it. I run down the aisle with a briefcase which I have printed out with a 'money in the bank' sticker (Money in the Bank is a WWE pay-per-view event in which the first person to climb to the top of a ladder and retrieve a briefcase gets the contract, to state they can challenge for the title belt at any time... I'm 37 years old by the way). I've got the briefcase, and I've handed it to the SLT member who is introducing me. I shout "I'm cashing it in!" and pick up one of the year 7 students and bodyslam him onto a high jump mat I've hidden behind a large table with a table cloth on it. I pick up the belt we have placed under his seat. The SLT looks at me as the music stops and I tell everyone that I don't know what came over me, she smiles and I continue with the assembly. The other members of staff look on in absolute disbelief, having no idea that this has been rehearsed and practiced, risk-assessed and assured so nobody would get hurt.

After the assembly, the SLT member asks me to speak to my lazy mate. He's another head of house. His activity in assembly was heads or tails. I speak to him about how he can encourage students to get involved more and do better, and he tells me in no uncertain terms that he doesn't care. Fair enough.

\* \* \* \* \* \*

I have been nominated for an award. No, I don't believe it either. A few teachers and parents have nominated me for an "Unsung Hero" award. It is an incredible yet unimportant honour to be nominated, and

I've invited my Mum to the ceremony. She loves all that stuff. My Mum, in short, is my hero. She's amazing. She worked at a primary school for the majority of her adult life, and has been commended with a life time achievement award for all she does for her school. I was always really envious of her ease in her job, and the respect she got from staff and students. I try my best to be like her, but like my Dad, I do this whilst drinking.

My Dad is great as well, don't get me wrong. He has shown me what it is to have fun; how to be a team player, and how to lead from the front. My Dad is a walking life lesson. A tough man; he is currently 70-odd years old and could still crush me like a fresh Ryvita. My Dad taught me to be spontaneous, and to treat the ones you love with surprises and acts of kindness. I'm so lucky to have them, and out of all of my friends parents, the only ones who are still together.

I remember one Christmas time, my Mum's school (which was a mile or so away from our house) always threw their Christmas tree away on the last day of term. My Mum always used to take it home, and we would reuse it for our Christmas tree. I was 14 or 15 when my Dad and I walked to the school to carry it home, as he didn't want to get pine needles in his recently-hoovered Mazda. Of course, I carried the heavy bottom end whilst my Dad carried the lighter top end. It was a good 9 ft tree. When we got back to the house I asked why I got the heavy end, and Dad responded with, "Because one day, you'll have an idiot son". I understood.

\* \* \* \* \* \*

My girlfriend (who is quickly becoming in the running to become my fiancee) has also been nominated for teacher of the year. This would be a massive deal as this award may actually mean something. She's not too keen on it, however. She's not one for speaking in front of people, and is quite shy, so the thought of winning an award in front of lots of people and having to speak, is really putting her off. If only she spoke in front of people for her day job…

\* \* \* \* \* \*

We have a presentation night at school (unrelated to the teaching awards) for kids who are getting their GCSE certificates. These things are awful. It's an awful lot of sitting and clapping for students to stand in a line and collect their certificate, and sit back down again. It is also catered for, and I am a bottle and half deep in red wine and at my funniest (in my head). The head of year walks on stage carrying a massive red notebook and I can't help but think she is the new presenter for "This Is Your Life".

Like a dogs need to bark, I sing out the theme tune. No laughs. Just looks.

The next morning I have been sequestered to the deputy head's office. I'm not sure if the head has lost interest in my shenanigans, or this is seen as a less major incident. I was fully prepared for a good dressing down. As I sat down, he looked at me with somewhat disappointment, and accused me of warbling the theme tune from "The Good, The Bad and The Ugly"! Whilst this would have been a lot worse, it would definitely have been much more funny. After I embarrassingly correct him, and explain she was carrying Michael Aspel's book, he rolls his eyes and says, "Look. You've been doing a lot better. You're a different person. Don't spoil it". I agree; this has been the best telling off ever.

## 34. Anything to declare?

Another trip away with the girlfriend, and this time we are off to Italy on a music tour. We are a little more on edge, as we've brought one of the naughtier year 8's. We were stuck between a rock and a hard place, as the school used the trip as a 'carrot' to improve his behaviour over the last few weeks. Of course, he was able to hold it together for this little while leading up to the trip. My fear is that this may lead to an implosion. When I say he is naughty, I mean he is a walking nuisance. It's not even good when he is quiet, as you know he is planning something. We go for a walk on night one, and pack up all our important documents and monies into a rucksack, as we haven't managed to get into our rooms yet, so no access to the safe.

We stop for ice cream and realisation has hit. The wallet is no longer with us. We retrace our steps, and find the wallet on top of a hedge. Thank goodness ; one of the teachers had put it on the floor to take a photo of her group. Clearly a kind passerby popped it on the hedge for us to collect.

However, on closer inspection, it is empty with probably close to £1000 missing. As my girlfriend is leading the trip, she has to contact police, claim on the insurance, and figure out what we are going to do (and keep her mouth shut in fear or giving the member of staff a good bollocking). It's a pain, and the poor girl spends a day in an Italian police station trying to explain the situation (Note: Italian police stations don't tend to have translators... or care about the fact they don't understand a word you are saying).

We've all chipped in with our staff expenses (we will stick with pasta instead of steak for the next few nights) and all students have their rightful amount of money, and off we go to a quaint little market for the students to buy trinkets and souvenirs for their families. Most of the students. Not the naughty kid. The little rebel has got on the coach with nunchucks (sold far and wide in Italy) and after a brief questioning, we are also in possession of the throwing stars (he's a pretty honest nuisance, if you ask me).

Items are swiftly confiscated, and we gently explain to him what an idiot he has been. He promises us that he has no more weaponry. Getting through customs with a 13-year old and a small arsenal would not go down too well. I feel assured that he has continued with his honesty streak, and the groups lead to rehearse for a concert. I hang back (not a fan of kid's out-of-tune ensembles) and give all the student rooms a quick sweep for any contraband, just in case.

It's a gun. I found a gun.

An incredibly realistic replica, yet fully functioning pellet gun. I confiscate this (obviously), and work out how to get rid of it. For now, I pop it in my rucksack as I'm a little late to the start of the concert, and I'm on support duty for any teary performers, and attaching music to stands (it's an open-air concert).

Of course, the students perform beautifully; the teachers are thrilled, students are elated, and the audience is full of joyful celebrations. Unfortunately, two wobbly-drunk locals have started dancing in front of the stage. The coach driver and I share a look, and we silently agree a plan of action, and start walking towards the front of the stage, to usher the clumsy dancers away from our students. The larger and scarier coach driver grunts to me, "If it comes to it, you take the big one!" I disappointingly agree... and suddenly remember that I have a gun in my rucksack. Thoughts rush past me of a possible altercation, Police checking my bag, and finding a gun, and everything starts to spiral. The two drunkards are shouting at the students on stage now, but the concert draws to a close without further incident, and teachers start whisking equipment and students away. Our tour guide is now around at the front, who speaks fluent Italian, and I ask her to interpret what they are shouting.

"Oh they were loving it. They were saying 'More! More! Ten out of ten! Ten out of ten!". Our best review yet. I skulk away quickly, giving the lads a grin on our departure.

We get back to the hostel and start our usual corridor monitoring with a couple of cheeky beers. The highlight for me was walking the PE teacher back in to reception with the gun against his head.

At Calais I walk next to "Il Naughty Signori" and I ask him if he has realised all his arsenal has gone. He claims he doesn't know anything about it. "I'm just going to tell them I've got a grenade". Now, I cannot say I'm proud of the next part, and it may be one of the dodgiest threats I've made, I whisper to the kid "If you try any shit I will get someone much bigger than you to fuck you up". He looks a little shocked, and sticks his jaw out and says, "You can't say that to me". I smirk. "Who are they going to believe? Me, a teacher? Or you, a little prick?". It works and I'm not proud. We make up after Dover security checks.

\*   \*   \*   \*   \*   \*

Back at school and its back to the grindstone. On lunch duties, I've been moved. My new area is controlling the queue to the "Grab and Go" food van in the playground. I subtly let the kids I like push in and mess about with a few of them. I love my duties. It's a moment where I'm not constantly with the most difficult students in the city, and feeling like I am constantly telling students off. I can talk to them about football, computer games, or whatever shit they are into.

At the end of my first duty, the two ladies at the food van ask me if I want anything, as it's all about to be thrown away. I take them up on their very kind offer. For the greater good of climate change, over the next six months I consume upwards of 240 tikka slices. I may ask to be moved back to the playground as I'm going to have to go to the DT department and get a new hole cut in my belt.

## 35. The Amazing Race

I may be the greatest head of house of all time. My house are back-to-back champions, and my assemblies are the talk of the school (in my head).

I have been asked by the headteacher to do five school assemblies to aid mental health alongside celebration week. I can't believe it. I would have loved to be part of the meeting where the mental health lead suggested I was the most appropriate person for the job.

This is going to be the assembly to end all assemblies. I want fire dancers, a steel band; imagine Cirque du Soleil, but in a venue unsuitable for 300 students, let alone fire breathing acrobats.

I've come up with a plan. I choose not to run it by anyone, as I don't want to be stopped.

I'm going to ask if everyone is ok. If you're not feeling ok, you're going to put your hand up, and I'm going to do my best to help you, live. (I have already set up two kids to put their hands up to help get the ball rolling). About five kids put their hands up and I ask them to go to the music block which is about 20 meters away, with my girlfriend waiting in there.

I have set up the ultimate 'happiness' room. We have an xBox set up, the music is flowing, and we have sweets, coke and balloons. The piece de resistance? My brother-in-law has brought in their brand new spaniel puppy.

By day five I have 200 hands go up. I am very proud, and the puppy loved the attention.

\*       \*       \*       \*       \*       \*

I've been asked to come up with an event which will help new year 7 students find their way around school and get involved in our enrichment activities. Luckily the PE teacher has got me hooked into "The Amazing Race", an American game\reality show where teams travel around the world completing fun tasks and winning prizes. A no-brainer really. With a month to go, I start doing some cryptic gorilla advertising, and start putting up QR codes around the school on the day of the event. If they scan these, they get a time boost.

I create stations dotted around the school, manned by older students or staff, and off go the year 7 groups, tossing pancakes, finding words in dictionaries, solving maths puzzles, putting up tents, and learning songs on xylophones, showcasing every department in the school. My creative juices are flowing now. I've brought this in to the modern world by giving each team an iPad with a stopclock, containing their map, and a camera to take photographs and videos as proof of their completion. "You're a god damn genius Gump!". I send them off on their tasks, and sit on a bench outside drinking coffee, chatting to the other heads of house.

This is the best idea I've had, and I tried to invent toilets with a stand for your phone.

## 36. ...... and he's gotta be fresh from a fight!

I won! I am the Unsung Hero of my district. It was an awesome ceremony and my parents and my sister attended. It's quite a long evening, with musical acts and a lot of speeches; best school, best teacher, best student: it's a lovely thing. After seeing the first award my heart drops. If you win, you are interviewed on stage and onto live local radio. They ask a few tricky questions, and I have realised that my headteacher is here too, so I will have to be professional at all times. It's so nerve-wracking that I refuse a top-up to my wine.

And the nominees are... me, a lady who has worked at a primary school for 30 years who is having time off due to her cancer, and another lady from a girl's school. I think to myself "Thank God... I'm not winning this".

"And the winner is....". Wow. That poor woman.

I start the long walk up the aisle to the stage, and I spot my headteacher. Her face has turned red and she is absolutely seething. Her hands are not even meeting in her clapping-type motion, and this kicks me up one more happiness notch. I thank my Mum and my girlfriend, and I'm asked some specific stories as to why I was nominated, and I was asked "Why do you do it?".

I wasn't really prepared for these questions, and clearly I want to be honest. I now know why people have words planned. I say about how much I love my school and my town, and I'm incredibly proud to be a part of both. I make the local paper on the back of this. As I return to my seat my Mum and Dad are very happy and my sister is crying, like a knob. Sadly my girlfriend doesn't win teacher of the year and loses out to someone who works with us who isn't fit to clean her boots. She is so relieved, after the questions that were asked of me. I think she knows her worth, regardless of an award. But I still like to wind her up about it and remind her now and again. She'll ask me about her curriculum design in music, and I'll reply with "Why don't you ask Frank in maths?". "Fuck off," she'll counter, and we continue our merry way.

I really think the world is at my feet at the moment and that this award could really take me places. I'm not sure where yet.

\*　　\*　　\*　　\*　　\*　　\*

Things are going so well, that a head of year job has come up, and I've applied for it. Not just that, I've been accepted for interview. There is just three of us up for the job, and I stand zero chance. My friend who runs the library is an applicant. He is outstanding, and does so much for the students here. There's also an art teacher who is great, will be great, but she's definitely young and inexperienced. Still; it's nice to have a change, and anything to keep me out of the behaviour room for the day.

It's your typical interview; you complete a written task, then you get interviewed by selected students whilst people take notes, and you finish off with an interview with the head and the SLT member who is in charge of heads of year. Unfortunately, there's no assembly section to the interview; there normally is, and I know I would be strong at this, so that's a shame. This would be a huge pay rise for me, and a lot of responsibility, but this will give me the opportunity to actually make bigger changes in peoples lives, and that's the pinnacle that I am aiming for. This is the first time this job has come up to non-teaching staff and I'm excited as to the direction my career could go now.

The interview goes great. I'm okay at the written task, smash the student panel, and for a change, I thought it went well with the head. The head's PA asks me for the first time ever through gritted teeth, if I would like a drink (our first positive interaction ever). "A cappuccino please", I've heard one of the women in the office say that these are notoriously hard to make in our kitchen and that the PA hates doing it. I more than hold my own throughout the process.

I leave the cappuccino.

After literally minutes of waiting, I'm informed they have given the job to the lovely young art teacher. Fair enough. I visit my mate in the library and offer my condolences; he looks to be annoyed. "Have you not heard?" He asks. "Another one of the heads of year and her mate have made a complaint that non-teaching staff would have too much time to run their year group well, so they thought it was only fair to give it to the teacher". I'm not as angry as he is (probably because I know he should have got the job over me), but I've asked for feedback and I'll get it in a couple of hours.

"So, we've decided to give it to the art teacher as she is a teacher and then she will be on an even keel with the other heads of year, but you did interview really well".

I'm slightly stunned that they've spoken the truth.

"Okay, but didn't you know that when we were all given an interview?".

"Well, there is a process that we need to go through before appointing people".

"Okay, so what can you do to get me ready for when the next head of year position comes up?" I ask with genuine interest and enthusiasm.

I kid you not, there are two minutes of silence. It's got to a stage where it is awkward and I'm happy when the deputy tells me that this is something they will definitely look into... they never did.

\* \* \* \* \* \*

There's a year 9 lad who I've been keeping a close eye on. He's the one whose Dad never said goodbye when sending him off for a week on adventure camp, and who I had on my shoulders at the disco. He's just got his second suspension. In our school, we have a 'three and you're gone' system; he is skating on thin ice. It's a shame. He is different kid nowadays, and an upstanding member of our school community. I've got him involved in house activities; he's a great kid. Every now and then I will pop into his lesson to see if he's okay. He is more than okay; he's great. His grades are improving and he's actively participating in lessons. It proves to me that the mentoring style I am using for him is working. Sadly, he's got suspended for getting in a fight outside of school, in our school uniform. The fight was unrelated to anything school wise, but the fact he was in uniform has been reported back to the school. Even though the two suspensions are three years apart, he has now had his strike two.

## 37. Oh the weather outside is frightful…

It's February half-term, and we're off to NYC again. This time it's not only cold, but it's snowing. It's beautiful, but cold. The wind still whistles down the avenues, but the beauty of the snow in Central Park makes it bearable.

I hang my group back a bit at a few crossings and wait for the other groups to get a bit ahead of us. I take my group in to Central Park for an almighty snowball fight. Frozen tears are falling with laughter and the students have a memory forever.

On arriving back at the hostel, a student has lost his wallet, and we go back and luckily find it. It's so pretty except, this mangey old cat we see scamper passed us. As we get closer it is the biggest rat you have ever seen.

Things have been going well and superbly timed, as always, and on one lovely day, we are off to ice-skate at the Rockefeller Center, surrounded by flags of the world. As staff, we don't participate, just in case one of us gets injured. With only five staff and 50 students, it's an exhausting trip. If we were down one member of staff, it would be a huge challenge and put us at risk of keeping the children safe. On this day, I finally get to go on the ice, but this is sadly because one of the students has fallen and hit his head. He's on the ice and has started fitting. It's a scary moment for all of us, and particularly when this lad has no medical history of seizures.

Thankfully, the seizure is short, and myself and the first aid crew from the rink are helping the boy off the ice. He is very confused, and doesn't respond. A rather annoyingly helpful lady follows us along, answering all the questions for the young lad, even though I'm only asking him the questions as to gauge his memory and understanding of where he is. "You are outside the Rockefeller on Sixth Avenue", she helpfully interjects. At this point I'm stressed, a bit scared, and I snap.

"Look! I'm not asking you am I? Why on fucking earth would I be asking you where you are? If I ask that question again I suggest your answer should be a long way away from here!"

As our staff team assemble and a plan of action goes into place to support the other 49 students as well as this poor lad, I go in the ambulance and begin the task of form-filling and contacting home and parents. I've come to get pretty good at this job. In this moment I feel quite lucky that I'm not leading the entire trip, and we have such a strong team of staff. With my girlfriend at the helm, leading the troops, everyone follows suit, and we trust each other to support one another to make the best decisions and keep us all safe and sane. This is the team that I excel in.

We are in hospital for many hours, receiving scans and tests. It's a great place, and would receive five stars on AirBnB if we were in the UK. We are waited on hand and foot, our room has a wide screen TV with wireless headphones, and I realise the lad is feeling better when he quietly says, "Sir? How fit are these nurses?" Now I can start to breathe.

I leave the hospital at 5am, when another member of staff comes to take over. We have a rota set up to give everyone some rest. We explain to the other kids that the lad is okay and he will be back with us soon. We don't tell them that he fractured his skull and there's a small hole 2mm from his jugular. We keep that piece of information for the parents and school only. The students have been absolutely amazing. They can see that we are worn ragged, we are stressed and worried, and they totally excel. They even come and check in on us, and bring us coffee! It brings a tear to your eye on an exhausting and emotional day. I adore them. I pop off on the shopping day to grab a quick lager, go down a side street, pass three bars which are closed, and then end up at a pokey little place called Judge Roy Beans. As I sit down at the bar I notice another member of staff three seats down. The odds are quite literally 10,000 to 1, but it's good to see someone else had the same thought.

Another staff change and the trip leader is at the hospital. She's been given the bill. From ice-skating to two nights in hospital, he has managed to spend $20,000 in hospital bills. $20,000! I could get Dr Dre for that. Thank God we always get full insurance.

It appears the hospital aren't too keen that we are flying home soon, and don't want to discharge our young lad. The trip leader is confused. The insurance company are saying that it's fine, the doctors are saying it's not. After a bit of digging, and gathering parent and child's viewpoint, we make a tentative decision that the hospital may just want to make the bill a bit higher, now they know we are getting a full payout. The insurance, parents and child give us full permission, and we discharge the student and get him out of the hospital, and fly him home. The hospital strongly suggest he should not sleep on the flight home. Shame it's a red-eye flight.

We get to JFK and discover the airline has oversold the flight and ten of our kids haven't even been given seat numbers. We realise that flights do this quite often; but it's rare to split up a school group full of children. We are back and forth with the airline, as they start getting on the tannoy, asking other passengers to give up their tickets so we can fill our quota and all get on the flight. It's been a very long and exhausting week, and this seems crazy to us. Eventually, they don't get enough tickets, and boarding has started. The airline staff sternly tell us to board the flight, and this is where I see my girlfriends true colours. It's a stand off. She has told our 50 students and five staff that we are not to board the plane, and that we refuse to board until our full group has tickets. She is absolutely right; it's a matter of safety for our students, and we cannot consider leaving ten behind! It's madness. The airline are in shock at the ballsy decision. We back each other, students and staff, are stand firm on our decision. I'm nearly in boyfriend-mode as the male member of staff starts to get irate and raises his voice at my partner. He's telling us that it is not specifically his fault and he is right, but I feel the need to remind him that he is the current face of a "stupid shit company". My girlfriend asks me to take a seat. She was probably right too.

As the plane is fully boarded, somehow, ten more seats are miraculously found, and we head home.

Back at school we are all commended for our heroism. You don't become an Unsung Hero for nothing.

          \*      \*      \*      \*

At school the new geography teacher is being commended in staff briefing for having 18 students turn up to rugby club and he could do with some more staff as there are only three of them.

I turn to the head of PE sitting next to me and say "I had 145 at year 8 football".

## 38. Frogger

My boss in the behaviour room has decided to call it a day and move to another school for more money. I'm suitably happy about this because I am next in line to the throne. I've kept my head down and I've paid my dues. I've worked hard and improved every aspect of my job and my life. It is about time, and I deserve it. I knew if I bided my time, the money would come.

\*       \*       \*       \*       \*       \*

It's a lovely weekend, and myself and two school colleagues have gone for a round of golf. We are on our way back, and driving through the town centre. When you work at a school you find yourself looking at groups of kids when you're in a car, to see if they are kids you may know.

As I look in the wing mirror behind me at this group of kids, one of them has stepped in to the road and has been hit and carried down the road on the bonnet.

It's horrible and so scary, and I'm out of the car and off down the road.

When I arrive she is conscious and in a lot of pain. She has a lot of damage to her upper leg where she's hit the road and skidded a good few meters. I'm just incredibly relieved that she is 7 out of 10 and not any worse. I'm on the phone to the ambulance as Mum arrives. It's helpful that I know the Mum and she is embraced in quite a sweet moment whilst on the phone to the emergency services. I'm asked to check on her and ask her if she knows my name. "Are you Sir from school?" I feel the fact that I'm on the scene isn't helping, and I imagine that the confusion is maybe making her think she has a head injury. My two mates are dealing with the incredibly shaken up driver who is in floods of tears. I ask the Mum if she is okay to take her daughter to hospital. She agrees and gives me a hug which makes me believe that she is feeling the worst moment of her life.

We decide to continue to help, and drive the lady in tears home. Another one of us take her car. Back at the house we get someone to look after her and she hands us her business card, just in case we need to contact her for anything. She's definitely in her 70's.

We get back in our car and start our journey home again, in a more subdued and quiet manner. We know that we've done well for everyone involved, and also the school.

My mate breaks the silence. "Why does she have a business card?"

A couple of seconds pass.

"I mean how many kids does she run over?"

When back at school, we discover the girl has escaped with minor injuries and needed some surgery to remove gravel from her bum. It could have been so much worse.

\* \* \* \* \* \*

We've started welcoming the prospective candidates for our new boss. Myself and the other woman I work with are both staying, and applying for the post, so we have a great opportunity to put new people off. We make sure to act tired and as if we are having a nightmare day. It's not hard to fake, as this is relatively near to the truth.

We also have a colleague who visits the school to work with some of our most troubling students, providing them with forms of therapy. She has informed us she is applying for the post too. This one makes me nervous. She is very, very good. There's another external candidate going for it, and then my 'lazy mate' who is currently working with the heads of year. I was surprised about his application. He doesn't really like kids, and loves shouting at them and belittling them. On second thoughts, there's no better place to do that, even though it's certainly not the ethos that I'm going for.

The interview process is another three-pronged attack, and I am ready for it. I'm nailed on for this. I've done my research. I know the job inside out. I just need to beat our therapist lady.

The interviews go so well. They shorten the field at lunchtime and I'm still in the running. The lady I work with has been eliminated and an external candidate. It's down to me, therapist lady and lazy-mate.

The day continues to go well. I absolutely nail my interview with the head. My ideas are hitting home, and I'm getting a lot of nodding heads and chewed glasses. I make a ten-minute presentation about the department and what I'd like to do with it. I walk out of the interview room with my head held high, as I know I couldn't have done any better. The stars are aligned and I'm getting my first pay rise in eight years. No more duties in the snow, no more making a big lunch to last five days. I might even be able to take my girlfriend on holiday and not just pay my half. More importantly, I can help these kids. I can really, really help them. They will have someone in their corner, they will thrive at school, and learn in a great atmosphere.

The day ends and I'm off to the football club to see some mates and wait for the good news. I'm celebrating.

An hour in and I get the call to say they've gone in another direction.

I choke back tears. I am truly gutted.

It shows me that the hard work and going the extra mile is not worth it. Doing unpaid work, sweating, bleeding and banging your head against the wall isn't worth it. That being the best person you can be isn't worth it. Winning awards isn't worth it. Just caring about your job isn't worth it. At the end of the day , whatever your bigger bosses deem appropriate, is what you will have to put up with, like it or not. I've been doing really well, but I know my self-destructive streak will get the better of me. I've waited eight years for this opportunity and in one day, it's over. All your hard work and improving yourself was for nothing... less than nothing. As now, I've got to walk home and tell my girlfriend that I didn't get it. I've got to walk around the school with all staff and students knowing that I wasn't good enough for the job. Do I wait a potential another eight years? It's embarrassing, and I can either like it or lump it. The therapy lady is nice though. I'll see how it goes and stop doing so much extra work  for a bit. For now, I think I won't go home just yet.

## 39. The Emperor has new clothes

I get a call from my Mum. Nan's died. I'm quite clearly emotional, and let my boss know that I don't really know what to do. She offers me to go home.

My Nan wouldn't have liked that. She wouldn't want me to do that; she was so incredibly caring and loving, she would be annoyed if someone needed my help and I wasn't there because I was at home feeling sad about her. My Nan once went on holiday to Sri Lanka and came home with one change of clothes as she had given most of her stuff away to locals. She was a true hero and I (and the world) will really miss her.

\* \* \* \* \* \*

The news has broke: who will be my new fearless leader?

It's my lazy mate.

I don't really know how to take this news.

It doesn't make me feel useless, I have already decided that I am useless. It's clear that he's kissed enough arse leading up to this point, and the head offers me a meeting to explain her decision. Looking back, I regret this next bit, but I was angry.

"If you are going to make decisions like that, you clearly don't know what you're doing, I'm okay for a meeting thanks!"

I hang up the phone and think "What have I done?".

There is no way he interviewed better than I did.

The other lady that I work with is equally upset, and is making her mind up on what to do. We go down the pub and have a chat about our options. Like it or lump it comes up again. We both decide that the students who access our room are going to need more help than ever. We question whether we really want to see everything we've worked hard for, go crumbling to the ground. We both decide to stay and work even harder.

Let's have it!

\*　　\*　　\*　　\*　　\*　　\*

Our boss leaves. We are more dejected about the guy coming in rather than her leaving. I have a little sob, and she thinks that's about her. So that's nice for her.

In September, we'll go again; working as hard as we can to give these kids a fighting chance. Just got to get this trip to Italy first with the football teams.

The Italy team consists of myself, the librarian, the PE teacher, the RE teacher (who is football mad) and the new head of drama) who I heard talking about Arsenal once, so he's worth a punt).

What a trip it is. Full of laughter and over-achieving kids. It's what it's all about.

On Trip Advisor, the hotel has just over one star, and we look forward to adding to their rating. We have three teams: two year 8 and one year 10. We play three games around Milan, with tours of the San Siro and a little walk around Milan. They also have two days of training with a newly promoted Seria A side. It's amazing, start to finish.

Our tour guide is fantastic and continuously sets up football quiz questions for us to make the journey quicker. The weather is good and I've got a single room, which is a massive rarity on these things.

On the first night, we notice there's another school group in the hotel. Their staff are incredibly loud and unprofessional. One of the staff enters our staff bedroom and starts talking to us. He is so drunk that he thinks it is his room, even though five staff sit inside it, surrounded by our stuff. We complain to one of the other female teachers from the school. "Thats nothing! Yesterday two of them weren't allowed on the boat trip, they were that bad!".

On a trip to the local cafe our PE teacher orders a lemon drink. I know in my head he thinks he is getting lemon Fanta. With my pigeon Italian, I know at no point that he is getting this, and the word Fanta is yet to be mentioned by either of them. A straight lemon juice arrives. Literally, 4 or 5 lemons have been juiced in to a glass and has been delivered to the table by an incredibly confused waiter. I know it doesn't sound much, but I have barely laughed at a single incident more. He takes a sip with quite a lot of the cafe staff watching and pulls a face of the Shelbyville resident who steals the lemon tree from The Simpsons. I will never not laugh at this.

We play Inter Milan's feeder club on day four, and they are amazing. It's like watching a flock of starlings change direction; all in fluid motions, and we are soundly stuffed. It's very rainy and the students are complaining that they are being called "fish and chips" by some of the opposition. I tell them that they will never get a better compliment; it means you are doing well. Why would you insult someone who isn't good at football, during a match?

Later on in the bar whilst the students get food, we have been told by our tour guide that Marco Materazzi is in the other bar. We (as staff) are very excited by this, and the PE teacher has concocted a plan where I film him pretending to head butt him. We set it up as his back is turned and as the PE teacher goes to do it our new friend Marco turns and wonders what is going on. We are all full of smiles and hugs, and the tour guide translates a conversation between us and him. Photos are taken with us and our teams, and we have an incredibly memorable night.

As we get on the coach, our translator says "he's not particularly tall for a goalkeeper is he?"

We then find out he was Inter Milan legend Francesco Toldo, and not recipient of Zidane's headbutt, Marco Materazzi. His non-understanding of a PE teacher pretending to head butt him now makes more sense.

He's incredibly embarrassed. I tell him to have a glass of lemon and shut up.

## 40. Every member of school staff has done this!

It's a new academic year, and the first house assembly of the year, so we are introducing the new year 7's to the house system. I have planned a decent assembly, starting with one of our really talented students playing some electric guitar, accompanied by his friend on drums, who happens to be from a different house.

It starts great, and he's swinging his guitar around and playing behind his head. He really is super-talented. I really hope he goes on to do great things in music.

Assemblies are only 15 minutes long but obviously takes a fair amount of planning. Unfortunately, they have gone over their allotted time, and it's getting close to four or so minutes. I start a round of applause and try to get them to stop and say thank you, but they continue to play over the top of me.

They go for ten minutes. I don't want to run on stage and start unplugging things and being angry; I feel like that it would ruin the appearance of the house system. I look to the SLT in charge of things. He doesn't know what to do either. When they finish the drummer shouts "Your house sucks! My house is better!" throws his drumsticks, and kicks over the drum kit.

Now! You reading this may think that is quite cool thing to do, but I will tell you something for nothing. It wasn't. It was a real dickhead move, done by a real dickhead kid.

After the assembly, a couple of the other heads of house come up and ask me what went on. "I'll tell you what went on... that kid is a fucking prick, I've been planning that assembly for two weeks".

They then point that I have a microphone around my neck. One lovely girl in year 7 has a cochlear implant and I've been wearing a small microphone around my neck for the last 45 minutes. I return to my office and wait for the call.

*   *   *   *   *   *

The PE department are desperate and have asked me to run a football team for one match, as they have contrasting fixtures, so I begrudgingly agree. It's on the 3G pitch, and quite a few of the kids have come down after school to watch the game. At half-time my striker seems a bit upset and I take him to one side to ask if he's okay. He tells me he is being racially abused by one of the kids in the crowd. I move over to the other side of the pitch and ask the oppositions manager if he has heard anything; he tells me he hasn't. I stand near enough to the crowd but not close enough so it looks like I'm there to listen.

It happens and I can't even bring myself to write here what was said. It's gross ,and I've jumped the fence as I've seen the boy who's said it, as he is mouthing the words. I tell them all to vacate the premises and go home, and they will all be hearing from me in the morning. They refuse to leave and I tell the referee to stop the game. I say we'll forfeit the game unless these kids leave. They all leave giving me a load of abuse. I check my striker is okay and ask him to talk to me after the game, if he is happy to do so.

The game finishes and I still have no idea what the score was. I speak to the manager of the other school and ask if he heard what was said and who said it . He confirms both things. The referee then joins in and says that he will have to include it in his report.

My brain says "Think of the headlines", but if this can stop this disgusting behaviour from happening again, then let's do it.

I write an email to the head of PE and SLT about this kids behaviour, and what was said; the fact that the school could even suffer a fine, and the follow-up needed to support the victim.

They investigate for less than a day, and in spite of witness reports the perpetrator gets a one-day exclusion. It's so much of a joke, I never coach a team again.

\* \* \* \* \*

She said "Yes" on a trip to Scotland for my sister's wedding. I've proposed and she's said "Yes". I genuinely can't believe she has! The fool!

## 41. The cuddle room?

As we predicted, our new boss is the worst possible person to have this job. Its like he's watched YouTube videos of Mr Bronson from Grange Hill and has decided, 'Yes, that's what I should be like'.

Our first meeting, and he has told us that we are moving away from the nice-nice approach, and that everyone calls our department 'the cuddle room'. This couldn't be any further from the truth, but hey-ho.

He continues to lay out his expectations of us. We are no longer allowed to use the office for paperwork, or have five minutes to have a sandwich; this is now his area, and no one else's. A bit weird, but we'll cope.

He advises we shouldn't have repeat offenders, and if anyone is getting sent here too often, it's up to us to make their lives hard, so they get kicked out.

I look at the lady who I work with, and we both just look down and shake our heads. We are in for a shock.

He wants our roles to change so rather than dealing with students in our department, he wants us permanently "out and about". We don't really know what this means, but it's been made clear that there is no wiggle room.

He has suggested that he will sit in the room, acting demon-ish to kids who probably get shouted at all day at school and home, and now we will do the same. We will be outside the room with no real direction so we don't really know what he is up to.

Its a bad meeting, and I've decided I may need a drink for the first time in a while.

\*     \*     \*     \*     \*     \*

I go to football that evening, and bump in to an old mate, whose son is at the school too. He doesn't get to see his son much sadly because of a difficult divorce. He thanks me profusely, and is really appreciative of what I've done for his son (going around his house to get him in for an exam, and helping him with homework at lunchtime).

This is really well timed, as I know what I'm doing is right and trying to get kids expelled from school is wrong.

\* \* \* \* \* \*

It's now gone around the students that we have a new leader in our department. The staff are fully aware, and many people are scratching their heads as I do. "I'm so sorry' from lots of staff. I feel like a loved one has died and I'm getting pity.

One of the heads of year is elated. I ask why she's so happy? "Well, he did fuck all in here! He's someone else's problem now". Great.

The kids are finding out now and they have some choice words about him too. I do really well to act professionally, and my new catch phrase is "because that is what the school has deemed the appropriate person".

They are right though. He is a knob.

On day two of his reign, we have four kids leave before the first bell has rung. He is quite proud of himself and has a big smug grin on his face. Myself and my colleague chase after the kids and try to get them back to our department; two walk off school site and the other two go back to the room. He decides to extend their time in the room for walking out. They both leave site as well.

\* \* \* \* \* \*

I've got a call from the deputy head to get down to his office, as one of the kids I mentor is in trouble. I rush down, and it's the kid I've taken under my wing.

He's looking at the floor, and he looks upset. The deputy tells me that he has got his final strike, for calling my new boss a fat cunt.

This is all my fault! My heart sinks.

The deputy explains the situation, and he's excluded. It's all because he thought he was doing the best thing for me.

I ask him why he did it, and he explains that my new boss was hassling him. My head immediately knows that he did this on purpose.

I walk with him to the gate and he takes his long walk home; to what, I don't know. We tried so hard together as a team, and a moment of madness has ruined his future.

I walk back to my department, holding back tears. I did my best for four years to help him to avoid these situations, and teach him to be the best person he can be. He listens, he reacts and he tries harder. He's an amazing kid who has a really tough home life, and I feel my boss has purposely wound him up to get a reaction from him.

I sit at my desk and need a minute. My boss comes out and asks me why I'm not "out and about", with a smug grin on his face. He knows. He definitely knows what he's done. I finish the day and know there is nothing I can do. I cry all the way to the pub and I have no memory of the next few days.

## 42. Good afternoon, good evening and goodnight.

I've deleted my 'boss' from all social media platforms. I don't need him talking to me about stuff I do outside of school as well.

His new favourite thing is to professionally tell me how horrible I am at my job via email at 8pm or 5am. I've asked him not to email me outside of working hours, but he continues to do whatever he wants.

He has an annoying trait of reading things off my phone from over my shoulder "Oh are you still mates with..." I've asked him more than once not to do this, and I know he is just making a point, as I'm on my phone.

It doesn't matter to him that I caught him watching two hours of the Tour de France on his phone last week, but he can do what he likes. He's untouchable.

The lady and I now start our day at the bottom of the stairs, as it's getting tiring walking up and down them, trying to get students back in the room after they have stormed out.

We meet at break time most days down in another block, as we aren't allowed in our department during the day. If we are seen getting a drink of water he will ask us why we aren't "out and about". My God, it's boring.

We have realised that we aren't really helping anyone anymore. The kids based in our department are either getting worse or getting expelled. Less kids are getting sent to us; in fact it is down 40%, as kids don't want to go there, which looks great on our data, annoyingly. Unfortunately students leaving school site is up 300%, but we don't have a spreadsheet for that.

We get back to our department at the end of the day to collect our stuff, and try and do some work in our allotted work hours.

"Tidy this place will you?" Is the normal call we get as he goes off to do something more important, like tidy his Duke of Edinburgh cupboard. Seriously. This must be the tidiest cupboard in the world. Or perhaps there's a good looking teacher down in the science block he's keeping an eye on.

We look around the room. Laptops shoved in cupboards with cables broken (we fought for three years to get these). Zero work completed by any student in there (students used to have to meet a certain amount of work in there, or repeat the day). We ask about this, but they are now concentrating on behaviour. Cough cough bullshit cough cough.

"All he's completed today are those two packs of penguins in the bin".

The lady I work with has a few things on her windowsill, such as teabags and some pens. "Oh, and tidy this shit up!" He bellows.

"I'm leaving; this is the opposite of what we should be doing," she says. "I thought you might," I say. "I won't be far behind you".

It's only a matter of time that a student does something really stupid because of what he is doing to them.

\*　　\*　　\*　　\*　　\*　　\*

Our boss has been granted access to the whole school CCTV. We use this to see if kids are lying, investigating acts of vandalism, or if there is a fight so we can see which kids have filmed it, and so on.

Our boss has another idea for this. He can now track myself and the lady I work with. I spend some time in the heads of year office as I can help out and chase up students, complete behavioural investigations with them, or discuss if there are any behavioural issues that can be addressed.

Our boss calls this office and asks us to get back "out and about".

I feel like I'm in the Truman Show.

I return to my office at the end of the day, with another day of achieving nothing under my belt. I hear him talking to another member of staff about my performance and the fact I'm "shooting myself in the foot". I walk in and tell him the list of jobs I've completed in the time he's talking about, and get my coat and go to the pub. My mental health is at an all-time low.

\* \* \* \* \* \*

Today we have been given a new list of students who need mentoring. There are 40 students names on there! We split the kids between the three of us, deciding on who we would work with best. We leave a few of the more challenging ones to our boss, as he's obviously the expert.

We meet to discuss this with him and he explains that we have got the wrong end of the stick and we will be mentoring 20 kids each. He will "oversee" the process. I don't know if you've ever mentored a student, but less is more. You can dedicate more time, get to know them better, and give them person-specific mentoring. With 20, it is not possible unless you were a full-time mentor, and there were two more hours a day to complete this.

I dread coming to work. I'm back to thinking about driving in to a tree again to get some time off. I don't see the point of any of this. I'm not a classroom assistant. I'm here to deal with behaviour, not stand in rooms I'm clearly not wanted.

I'm drinking more so I can sleep and forget.

## 43. A fresh start is as good as a change...

She's handed her notice in. The lucky thing. She's got a job in a call centre or something along those lines. She's dedicated and great with students and staff, but can no longer go on, not making a difference.

She hands her notice in and I'm annoyed that I haven't found another job yet. Our boss reacts to this by taking his feet off his desk at the end of the day when we return, and hiding his phone which had the test match streaming.

I request a meeting with the deputy head, so I can ask him a few questions. Why is it okay for my boss not to do any work? I'm assured he has the job due to his managerial experience. Wow. Really? It was in a bank wasn't it? Those poor people. This doesn't satisfy me at all, but I'm glad

I've started to report his dangerous behaviour.

I get an email at 6am explaining to me what I'm doing wrong in my job, and I forward it to the deputy. I don't get a reply.

It's so sad that it has come to this. I hate the job I love, I hate the school I love, I hate the life I love. I need to do something sharpish or I could end up in a lot of trouble; alcoholism, or assault charges.

Try harder to find new work, and have an interview at a rival school. Fingers crossed!

\*     \*     \*     \*     \*     \*

I visit the deputy head the day before my interview, and ask if the door will still be open to me to return if I do choose to leave. I don't really want to go to another school. I love this school too much. He tells me that the the door is always open to good people.

I know how to take this, and it isn't positively.

\* \* \* \* \* \*

The interview goes well. The school is quite far from me, but you can't put a price on mental health. I get the call to say I came second and I won't be offered the job.

It's disappointing but understandable; I even got recognised from the awards night.

My boss asks how it went, and I tell him that I didn't get it "So I'm stuck with you, am I?". I fucking hate him. I've started documenting all unprofessionalism from him, as I'm getting overly tired of it now.

It's time for the appraisals, and it's not going well. I ask to stop the meeting and ask for someone else to be in the room for this, as I felt so uncomfortable with the way he was behaving. The next day, the deputy head obliges, and the meeting has taken on a whole new format. It seems to go reasonably well. Funny that. At one point I'm called selfish as I want to go home on time, and then he goes on to say I'm too selfless at times. Your guess is as good as mine.

I brought up that my boss keeps trying to get me to work in different departments and it's unprofessional, and not part of my job description. It's met with silence from both.

Its okay though; the music trip is soon and I haven't missed one of these in six years. We are going to Austria, and I'm well versed on the Sound of Music.

I get an email later on, with the notes made from the appraisal meeting. It's not accurately depicting the meeting, but who do I tell? Who would listen.

I read another email from the boss. We have a student in tomorrow, and "if we make it hard for him in the morning he will probably walk out, and we won't have to deal with him." I forward this to the deputy head.

* * * * * *

My girlfriend is now a head of year, and we've got a really enthusiastic and genuinely lovely new head of department in music. She's so pleased to hear that we have a strong team set up for music tours, as this will be the first one she's running, and we are all confident that we can support her.

She's had to advise me that I'm no longer on the trip. I'm shocked and really saddened, as I feel I must have done something to upset her. She reassures me that's not the case, but she's been told from the behaviour manager, that he won't approve of me going on the trip, as I should be, 'concentrating on this job right now'. I am absolutely fuming. How dare he? I've been doing this job longer and better than he has, and he's using his 'managerial skills' to manage me out of a job. I can see exactly what he's doing, and purely because I don't agree with his ethos. Purely because, I care about the kids. I don't want them kicked out of school so they 'aren't our problem any more'. Some of these children have the worst home lives, and come to school to feel normal. Of course they get into trouble, and they need someone to look after them, to look up to, and to be a role model for their future. They don't need another adult that shouts at them and forces them to feel unsafe. I feel like I'm taking crazy pills. I haven't put a foot wrong and have been working even harder to try and get students to stay in school. Clearly he doesn't like that.

I've led, supported on, and accompanied about 40-50 school trips in the time I have been here, across the world. I know I'm good at it, and I know I would be a strength to their team. This is the first one I've ever been told I can't go on. I've even been on ones I didn't want to go on. I even won a poxy award.

\* \* \* \* \* \*

A student is really kicking off in our room, when I return to grab a protein bar. Apparently my boss (who is taller and fatter than me) has pinned him to the wall by his collar and tie. I tell the student to report it to the safeguarding lead as no one will believe me.

He does. Nothing happens.

\* \* \* \* \* \*

Another incident has come to light. He has told a student in the main room to sit properly multiple times. He has then laughed at her when she cried, and she's now walked out. This is the second day of her being missing from home and school, and we are all worried.

Thankfully day three and we get the call to say she has returned home.

After a week of more horse shit, he takes me to one side and offers for me to leave the department again.

This time to save my mental health, I agree.

## 44. Cover me!

I meet with HR and work out my contract to move sideways (downwards) to be a cover teacher. I have no idea what I'm getting myself into, but I know things can't get any worse.

My new boss is nice, and is also about ten years younger than me. I sit in the staff room, in the knowledge that I am safe and I can't take any more of a beating from him.

The first morning as a cover teacher, and I'm looking through my timetable to see what I will be doing today. I hear an almighty crash from my old department (it's next to the staff room) and someone shouting, "You lot are taking the piss!". I look through the external window to see a young girl walking off crying. I later bump in to her and ask her if she's okay, and she tells me she had forgotten her tie.

I cover a couple of lessons that morning, and everything feels more positive and upbeat. I hadn't even thought about where my next scolding, derogatory email or nasty comment was going to come from. Sadly, it came from the last place I expected; the kids.

I never thought I'd have problems with them, and yet here I am, sitting in a room surrounded by carnage. Glue sticks, pens and whatever else isn't attached is getting thrown around. I sit at my desk with my head in my hands. I have lost.

\* \* \* \* \* \*

Being a cover teacher is tough work! Students have no interest in doing anything you ask, and teachers expect that the work is completed. There is no training to become a cover teacher, no teaching strategies or qualifications or provided, no help comes your way. You are just thrown in with a bunch of kids, and hope that you make it back out alive. The subject departments are often so busy that they don't come in and check up on you, and if you report poor behaviour, it's too late to do anything about it, and they are too busy to deal with the aftermath anyway. This continues for the first two months; no break and no help. I don't feel I can even call the behaviour room to collect students; I couldn't bear to have that smug prick turn up.

Cover teaching is the worst job there is. It makes you think less of yourself and your own abilities. Imagine if you will, going on holiday and just walking up to a group of lads around a swimming pool and saying, "Right everyone, we're going to learn about Pythagoras' theorem today". Imagine that look they would give you, followed by the laughter. It would be demeaning; especially if that was your only job of the day.

On one day I get hit squarely on the back of the head with a pen. I just ignore it, but it certainly makes me bow my head a little lower.

Another day, kids are squirting water at each other from the taps in the science lesson. I am a broken man, and my mental health is now at an all time low. I have no escape; I can't quit as I would lose my home. I can't get help. I can't have time off, I can't retrain, I can't think or breathe; I've had enough, and some seriously dark thoughts enter my mind.

I wouldn't have to do this anymore, and I wouldn't have to deal with the fall out of quitting. There would just be nothing but sweet, blissful nothingness. I wouldn't have to feel like this anymore. I wouldn't have to let anyone down anymore. I wouldn't have people feeling sorry for me, or laughing at me for not getting that job. I wouldn't have people checking on me. I am truly, truly broken.

I've had these thoughts before, during my time here; but it's getting more worrying.

I'm beginning to plan it and weigh up the pros and cons of different ways to go.

I have a particularly bad lesson, and the students are almost feral. They won't sit down. They won't be quiet, and they won't listen. I am just a void; a scarecrow getting in the way of their good time. I am no good at this. I am no good at anything.

The time comes to end the lesson, and I tell the students they can leave. They are so rowdy that they can't hear me. I raise my voice slightly, and tell them the same thing, but they don't even look at me.

I pick my bag up and I leave.

\*   \*   \*   \*   \*   \*

I've been called to the head's office as soon as I get in. Before school is normally when the worst meetings happen. I get grilled about yesterday's lesson where I just walked out.

I explain my troubles through watery eyes; the fact that I have lost. I'd been holding on and holding on, but the time has come for me to get help. I'm in a bad place, I'm at the bottom of the well, and no one is coming to help. I'm terrible at this job, and truly I've never got over the fact I didn't get promoted after working so hard, and the fallout that followed.

The head moves forward in her chair and says,

"It sounds like you want me to end your contract".

I swear to you this is what she thought was an appropriate response.

Thats exactly what you want when you're drowning; a foot on your head.

I ask if I can leave the meeting, and they allow me to do so. I was a little shocked by her comment. I thought they may have been more supportive. It sounds like she's jumping two-footed into getting me to leave. It seems quite reminiscent of the way they get the kids to leave too. Just keep kicking them and they'll eventually go. Not your problem any more.

I go to the bathroom and sit on the toilet. I hold my head in my hands, and I finally decide that tonight will be the night to end it all.

I finish work and I go to the pub; half to get up the courage, and half to avoid everyone who loves me. I drink a lot, and I get home and try to write my note. I want everyone to know that this is exactly what the head teacher said to me, when I was asking for help. I film myself on my phone, as I'm too drunk to write. I've got vodka, and a lot of pills.

I film and cry. I drift off to sleep.

## 45. The End

I awake on my sofa. I was too drunk and too much of a pussy to actually go through with it. Another thing I'm terrible at.

Through the haze, I decide that enough is enough I'm through with feeling like this. My life hasn't ended. I decide in this moment to give my life to others. I will dedicate it to helping people who are in need, and not to people who don't deserve it. I will never say no, and I will never stop.

I write my notice and I hand it in. I don't even care if the head thinks she's won. She's a selfish, egotistical and manipulative cow, and she always will be ugly inside and out.

I speak to my fiancée and ask her what she thinks about moving away? I see the look of relief in her eyes, and the weight on her shoulders is easing. I had no idea that my pain was hers, too.

## EPILOGUE

Life is a lot better. In fact, life is good!

You may not believe some of this but I'm two years sober, I have a better job in the care sector, and I'm on a lot more money than I was at school. I live in a little village with my wife and two cats, I sit outside most mornings and chat to people on their walks.

I've got a work-life balance (my golf handicap is coming down by the week which is great, and slightly annoying for all the club tournaments I play in).

I'm happily married to the music teacher who has also gone on to do amazingly in her new role as an SLT member in a role she never would have been offered at our old place. She still hasn't forgiven me because on our cotton wedding anniversary I got her a signed photo of June Brown.

We've been married five years would you believe... that lucky woman!.

Obviously its not all Refresher bars and roses. I still have sleepless nights, I've been to see my GP and she said that the feelings I am describing towards my old job and headmistress is borderline PTSD. I still have nights thinking about "Why didn't I say that?", "Why didn't I walk out of that meeting?", "Why didn't I tell her what was really going through my mind?". I'm basically just learning to live with it and I'm glad I'm out of such a poisonous environment.

I still speak to the odd person from the school and I get the odd message off students asking how I am and asking what I'm up to (it's a little bit weird). I always tell people that I'm happy now, which is a new sensation, and also when someone tells me "Well done" I'm getting better at replying "Thank you," rather than thinking I disagree.

I still get sinking feelings whenever my boss wants to talk to me but it's always been positive in the care industry. "We really appreciate what you're doing". "Thank you so much for helping out". "Well done on how you handled that situation". It's never "I hear you high-fived a service user and I've rang the police!".

Thank you for reading this. I do appreciate it. I really do... you didn't have to but you've made a sober, 40-year old (good husband, average golfer, terrible writer) very happy.

I appreciate you and I'll leave you with a few thoughts.

If you're unhappy, do something about it,. Don't be scared to ask for help. If you think no one cares... remember I care. I care about you and I want you to do well and I want you to be healthy in your mind. If you hurt your leg, you would probably see a doctor. Why wouldn't you do the same for your mental health?

If you work in a school and you're unhappy... LEAVE. If you feel unappreciated.... LEAVE. The only way a bully can win is if you let them.

I speak to staff who have left the school and this one phrase always gets said.

"The grass is so much greener".

Printed in Great Britain
by Amazon

19002868R20183